# GREAT INDIAN SPEECHES *for* CHILDREN

# GREAT INDIAN SPEECHES for Children

Introduction by

DERERK O'BRIEN

talking CUB

TALKING CUB
Published by Speaking Tiger Publishing Pvt. Ltd
4381/4, Ansari Road, Daryaganj
New Delhi 110002

First published in Talking Cub by Speaking Tiger in 2018



ISBN: 978-93-88070-63-8
eISBN: 978-93-88070-64-5

10 9 8 7 6 5 4 3 2 1



Typset in Libre Baskerville by Jojy Philip
**Printed at Gopsons Papers Ltd.**

# CONTENTS

# INTRODUCTION

As I sat down to write this, I started thinking, why do we need to have a book of speeches? In this day and age of round-the-clock access to the wonders of the Internet, where every speech and utterance by anyone can be viewed by millions at just a click, how will a book like this help? I thought some more, and here is what I concluded. A speech becomes great when it is not just applauded at that moment by the audience listening to it right then, but when it has been written and crafted and delivered by the speaker to such effect that it lives on in public memory. Such a speech needs to be not just heard, but also read. A great speech will consist of sentences and phrases that will resonate so deeply with the listener or reader that on seeing those words printed on a page even a century or more later, their impact can still be felt.

There are speeches that give us goose bumps each time we hear them, for example, our first Prime Minister Jawaharlal Nehru's speech as India stood at the threshold of becoming a free country: 'Long years ago, we made a tryst with destiny...' Seeing these words, hearing them in my head, my mind flies to that midnight hour when we awoke to 'life and freedom'. The years of struggle that our leaders and every Indian put in to win this freedom, the hopes of a whole country, the birth of a nation, are what I think about each time I read or listen to that speech. Nehru's words remain the promise to which we all must turn to every now and then and remember the pledge we made to ourselves as we became independent.

There are speeches that are remarkable for their newness of thought and wisdom. Swami Vivekananda's speech where he addressed the world as brothers and sisters and then went on to bring Indian and Hindu thought on the world stage, explaining the depth of its philosophy through simple words, can be read even today by people of all ages. Mother Teresa's Noble Prize acceptance speech, in which she talks about why we should give to the poor and the dispossessed and also how we need to keep giving till it hurts, encompasses the principles by which she lived her life and are the bedrock of the Missionaries of Charity organization.

In talking about the kind of society and nation we are and can become, the words of Mahatma Gandhi and B.R. Ambedkar should be read with great care and attention. The two leaders differed with each other on many things, yet what was undeniable was their unflinching love and concern for India. In his 1916 Banaras Hindu University speech, Gandhi talked about how poverty is all pervasive in the country, and yet that does not stop the ostentation of our ceremonies. He spoke bluntly of how we build beautiful places of worship and yet don't take care to keep the surroundings clean and healthy, which, unfortunately, continues to remain true to this day. B.R. Ambedkar, in his 1949 speech, took a close, hard look at the nation as it adopted the Constitution, and spoke frankly on how democracy can survive and should survive in India. He pointed out the importance of the Constitution and his words need to be read and understood by every Indian young and old even today, so we can live by the thoughts and principles that created the Constitution and safeguard against any attempts to alter it in fundamental ways.

Speeches by Subhash Chandra Bose, Balgangadhar Tilak, Dr Radhakrishnan and Rajendra Prasad present different facets of the freedom struggle and teach us about patriotism in varied ways. Tilak's words, 'Freedom is my birthright', became a rallying cry for freedom fighters across the country. Reading the speech in which he declared it for the first time, helps us understand the depth of his passion and commitment to the cause of freedom.

I am glad this book contains speeches that have been made in contemporary times too. Through them, one gets a glimpse of our country as it has grown and spread its wings in diverse areas. A.P.J. Abdul Kalam was a beloved personality and reading his thoughts on his teachers made me think of many of mine, and how teachers can change the very course of our lives. Subroto Bagchi speaks movingly of his growing up days in Odisha, and of his parents and the wings they gave him so he could think of kissing the world. I had heard Rahul Dravid's Bradman Oration when he delivered it in Canberra in 2011. Reading Dravid's own calm yet passionate feelings about the game, brought back to me all the reasons why cricket remains India's favourite sport. It is a speech that can bring tears to the eyes, whether you are a sports lover or not. Azim Premji, who not only built one of modern India's most successful businesses but has become one of the country's biggest philanthropists, shows us that the pursuit of wealth cannot be an end in itself. Nobel laureate

Amartya Sen's speech about the importance of basic education and how the lack of access to education is a form of violence in itself should be read by every young person who wants to understand the workings of human society. I was delighted to come across Ruskin Bond's gentle words on his love of books. When great loneliness strikes us, as it is bound to at any time in our lives, books are the companions that can comfort and bring perspective.

In the end, what do we learn about making a great speech after reading this book? That a great speech comes from conviction. You need to believe in what you are saying to make others believe you. It is also about preparation. A great speech needs to be nurtured and prepared. Yes, there are some truly wonderful extempore speeches too. Nehru's 'The Light Has Gone Out of Our Lives' speech, announcing the assassination of Mahatma Gandhi, was one such. But then it came from the deepest parts of his heart and he spoke what a nation was feeling at the time. But mostly, a good speech is one on which you have spent time—thinking and preparing and sharpening each word so that it finds its mark. A great speech is also obviously about oration. You need to be confident, stand up straight, project your voice and through your body language convince your audience that they need to not only hear you, but they need to listen attentively to each word and nuance.

*Great Indian Speeches for Children* is a book that will kindle the love of enquiry and debate among young readers, and in fact in readers of all ages. I enjoyed it thoroughly. Civilized debate as against ugly shouting matches, thoughtful words as opposed to empty rhetoric, moments of quiet contemplation instead of constant social media chatter—these are things we need more of in our lives. With this book, we get a bit of all these. Read, think, be curious, question—that is what makes us worthy individuals.

With every good wish,

**Derek O'Brien**

## SWAMI VIVEKANANDA

### Sisters and Brothers of America

*Chicago, 1893*

*Swami Vivekananda (1863–1902), a disciple of Ramakrishna, was one of the most influential spiritual figures in India. He represented India at the first ever World Parliament of Religions held in Chicago in September 1893. Here, Vivekananda delivered a speech which highlighted the principles of universality and inclusivity in Hinduism.*

Sisters and Brothers of America,

It fills my heart with joy unspeakable to rise in response to the warm and cordial welcome which you have given us. I thank you in the name of the most ancient order of monks in the world. I thank you in the name of the mother of religions, and I thank you in the name of millions and millions of Hindu people of all classes and sects.

My thanks also to some of the speakers on this platform who, referring to the delegates from the Orient, have told you that these men from far-off nations may well claim the honour of bearing to different lands the idea of toleration. I am proud to belong to a religion which has taught the world both tolerance and universal acceptance. We believe not only in universal toleration but we accept all religions as true.

I am proud to belong to a nation which has sheltered the persecuted and the refugees of all religions and all nations of the earth. I am proud to tell you that we have gathered in our bosom the purest remnant of the Israelites, who came to Southern India and took refuge with us in the very year in which their holy temple was shattered to pieces by Roman tyranny. I am proud to belong to the religion which has sheltered and is still fostering the remnant of the grand Zoroastrian nation.

I will quote to you, brethren, a few lines from

a hymn which I remember to have repeated from my earliest boyhood, and which is every day repeated by millions of human beings:

*'As the different streams having their sources in different places all mingle their water in the sea, so, O Lord, the different paths which people take through different tendencies, various though they appear, crooked or straight, all lead to Thee.'*

The present convention, which is one of the most august assemblies ever held, is in itself a vindication, a declaration to the world of the wonderful doctrine preached in the Gita:

*'Whosoever comes to Me, through whatsoever form, I reach them; all are struggling through paths which in the end lead to Me.'*

Sectarianism, bigotry, and its horrible descendant, fanaticism, have long possessed this beautiful earth. They have filled the earth with violence, drenched it often and often with human blood, destroyed civilization and sent whole nations to despair. Had it not been for these horrible demons, human society would be far more advanced than it is now. But their time is come; and I fervently hope that the bell that tolled this morning in honour of this convention may be the death-knell of all fanaticism, of all persecutions with the sword or with the pen, and of all uncharitable feelings between persons wending their way to the same goal.

## SAROJINI NAIDU

### The Hand That Rocks the Cradle Is the Power That Rules the World

*Calcutta, 1906*

*Best known as a poet, Sarojini Naidu (1879–1949) was one of the most prominent leaders of the Indian freedom movement. She was the first woman President of the Indian National Congress and the first woman Governor of independent India. Following are excerpts from a speech she delivered at the Indian Social Conference in Calcutta in December 1906. In this speech, she spoke about the importance of women's education in India.*

It seems to me a paradox, at once touched with humour and tragedy, that on the very threshold of the twentieth century, it should still be necessary for us to stand upon public platforms and pass resolutions in favour of what is called female education in India—in all places in India, which, at the beginning of the first century, was already ripe with civilization and had contributed to the world's progress radiant examples of women of the highest genius and the widest culture. But as by some irony of evolution the paradox stands to our shame, it is time for us to consider how best we can remove such a reproach, how we can best achieve something more fruitful than the passing of empty resolutions in favour of female education from year to year.

At this great moment of stress and striving, when the Indian races are seeking for the ultimate unity of a common national ideal, it is well for us to remember that the success of the whole movement lies centred in what is known as the woman question. It is not you but we who are the true nation-builders. But it seems to me that there is not even a unanimous acceptance of the fact that the education of women is an essential factor in the process of nation-building. Many of you will remember that, some years ago, when Mrs Satthianadhan first started *The Indian Ladies' Magazine*, a lively correspondence went on as to whether we should or should not educate our women. The women themselves with one voice pleaded their own cause most eloquently, but when it came to the man, there was division in the camp. Many men doubtless proved themselves true patriots by proving themselves the true friends of education for the mothers of the people. But others there were who took fright at the very word. 'What,' they cried, 'educate our women? What, then, will become of the comfortable domestic ideals as exemplified by the luscious "halwa" and the savoury "omelette"?' Others, again, were neither 'for Jove nor for Jehovah,' but were for compromise, bringing forward a whole syllabus of compromises. 'Teach this,' they said, 'and not that.'

But, my friends, in the matter of education you cannot flay thus far but no further. Neither can you say to the winds of Heaven 'Blow not where ye list,' nor forbid the waves to cross their boundaries, nor yet the human soul to soar beyond the bounds of arbitrary limitations.

The word education is the worst misunderstood word in any language. The Italians, who are an imaginative people, with their subtle instinct for the inner meaning of words, have made a positive difference between instruction and education and we should do well to accept and acknowledge that difference. Instruction being merely the accumulation of knowledge might, indeed, lend itself to conventional definition, but education is an immeasurable, beautiful, indispensable atmosphere in which we live and move and have our being. Does one man dare to deprive another of his birthright to God's pure air which nourishes his body? How, then, shall a man dare to deprive a human soul of its immemorial inheritance of liberty and life?

And yet, my friends, man has so dared in the case of Indian women. That is why you men of India are today what you are: because your fathers, in depriving your mothers of that immemorial birthright, have robbed you, their sons, of your just inheritance. Therefore, I charge you, restore to your women their ancient rights, for, as I have said, it is we, and not you, who are the real nation-builders, and without our active co-operation at all points of progress, all your Congresses and Conferences are in vain. Educate your women and the nation will take care of itself, for it is true today as it was yesterday and will be to the end of human life that the hand that rocks the cradle is the power that rules the world.

## JAGDISH CHANDRA BOSE

Temples of Learning

*Madura, 1915*

*Professor Jagdish Chandra Bose (1858–1937) was a pioneering physicist who studied radio and microwave optics. Through an experiment involving radio waves, he proved that plants too can feel. The following is a speech he delivered in Madura, Tamil Nadu, on 14 June 1915, on his way back to Calcutta from the Fourth Scientific Deputation to the West.*

In travelling all over the world—which I have done several times—I was struck by two great characteristics of different nations. One characteristic of certain nations is living for the future. All modern nations are striving to win force and power from Nature. There is another class of men who live on the glory of the past. Now what is to be the future of our nation? Are we to live only in the glory of the past and die off from the face of the earth, or to show that we are worthy descendants of the glorious past and to show by our work, by our intellect and by our service that we are not a decadent nation? We have still a great and mighty future before us, a future that will justify our ancestry. In talking about ancestry, do we ever realize that the only way in which we can do honour to our past is not to brag of what our ancestors have done but to carry out in the future something as great, if not greater, than they? Are we to be a living nation, to be proud of our ancestry and to try to win renown by continuous achievements?

These mighty monuments that I see around me tell us what has been done till very recent times. I have travelled over some of the greatest ruins of the Universities of India, I have been to the ruins of the University of Taxila in the farthest corner of India, which attracted the people of the West and the East. I had been to the ruins of Nalanda, which invited all the West to gain knowledge under its intellectual fostering. I had been all there and seen them. I have come here also and I want to visit Conjeevaram. But are you to foster the dead or try to bring back your University in India and drag once more from the rest of the world, people who would come down and derive knowledge from India? It is in that way and that way alone, [that] we can win our self-respect, and we can make our life and the life of the nation worthy.

The present era is the era of Temples of Learning. In order to erect Temples of Learning we require all the offerings of our mighty people. We want to erect temples and viharas, which are so indispensable to the study of Nature and her secrets. It is a problem which appeals to every thoughtful Indian. It is by the effort of the people and by their generosity that all these mighty temples arose; and now are we to worship the dead stones or are we to enact living temples so that the knowledge that has been made in India shall be perpetuated in India? I receive requests from the different Universities in America and Germany to allow students from those countries to come and learn the science that had its birth in India. Now is the knowledge to pass beyond our boundaries, so that again in future time we have to go to the West to get back this knowledge or are we to keep this flame of learning burning for all time?

## MAHATMA GANDHI

### Banaras Hindu University Speech

*Banaras, 1916*

*Mohandas Karamchand Gandhi (1869–1948), also known as Mahatma Gandhi or Bapu, was the political and spiritual leader of India's independence struggle. After training as a barrister, he spent twenty years in South Africa, where he developed the concept of satyagraha and fought for the rights of the Indians settled there. He returned to India in 1915. A year later, on 4 February 1916, he was invited by Madan Mohan Malviya to speak on the occasion of the inauguration of the Banaras Hindu University. Following are excerpts from the speech, in which he emphasized the need for Indians to develop awareness and proper conduct.*

The Congress has passed a resolution about self-government, and I have no doubt that the

All-India Congress Committee and the Muslim League will do their duty and come forward with some tangible suggestions. But I, for one, must frankly confess that I am not so much interested in what they will be able to produce as I am interested in anything that the student world is going to produce or the masses are going to produce. No paper contribution will ever give us self-government. No amount of speeches will ever make us fit for self-government. It is only our conduct that will fit us for it. And how are we trying to govern ourselves?

I want to think audibly this evening. I do not want to make a speech and if you find me this evening speaking without reserve, pray, consider that you are only sharing the thoughts of a man who allows himself to think audibly, and if you think that I seem to transgress the limits that courtesy imposes upon me, pardon me for the liberty I may be taking. I visited the Vishwanath temple last evening, and as I was walking through those lanes, these were the thoughts that touched me. If a stranger dropped from above on to this great temple, and he had to consider what we as Hindus were, would he not be justified in condemning us? Is not this great temple a reflection of our own character? I speak feelingly, as a Hindu. Is it right that the lanes of our sacred temple should be as dirty as they are? The houses round about are built anyhow. The lanes are tortuous and narrow. If even our temples are not models of roominess and cleanliness, what can our self-government be? Shall our temples be abodes of holiness, cleanliness and peace as soon as the English have retired from India, either of their own pleasure or by compulsion, bag and baggage?

I entirely agree with the President of the Congress that before we think of self-government, we shall have to do the necessary plodding. In every city there are two divisions, the cantonment and the city proper. The city mostly is a stinking den. But we are a people unused to city life. But if we want city life, we cannot reproduce the easy-going hamlet life. It is not comforting to think that people walk about the streets of Indian Bombay under the perpetual fear of dwellers in the storeyed building spitting upon them. I do a great deal of railway travelling. I observe the difficulty of third-class passengers. But the railway administration is by no means to blame for all their hard lot. We do not know the elementary laws of cleanliness. We spit anywhere on the carriage floor, irrespective of the thoughts that it is often used as sleeping space. We do not trouble ourselves as to how we use it; the result is indescribable filth in the compartment. The so-called better class passengers over we their less fortunate brethren. Among them I have seen the student world also; sometimes they behave no better. They can speak English and they have worn Norfolk jackets and, therefore, claim the right to force their way in and command seating accommodation.

I have turned the searchlight all over, and as you have given me the privilege of speaking to you, I am laying my heart bare. Surely we must set these things right in our progress towards self-government. I now introduce you to another scene. His Highness the Maharaja who presided yesterday over our deliberations spoke about the poverty of India. Other speakers laid great stress upon it. But what did we witness in the great pandal in which the foundation ceremony was performed by the Viceroy? Certainly a most gorgeous show, an exhibition of jewellery, which made a splendid feast for the eyes of the greatest jeweller who chose to come from Paris. I compare with the richly bedecked noble men the millions of the poor. And I feel like saying to these noble men, 'There is no salvation for India unless you strip yourselves of this jewellery and hold it in trust for your countrymen in India.' I am sure it is not the desire of the King-Emperor or Lord Hardinge that in order to show the truest loyalty to our King-Emperor, it is necessary for us to ransack our jewellery boxes and to appear bedecked from top to toe. I would undertake, at the peril of my life, to bring to you a message from King George himself that he expects nothing of the kind.

Sir, whenever I hear of a great palace rising in any great city of India, be it in British India or be it in India which is ruled by our great chiefs, I become jealous at once, and say, 'Oh, it is the money that has come from the agriculturists.' Over 75 per cent of the population are agriculturists and Mr Higginbotham told us last night in his own felicitous language, that they are the men who grow two blades of grass in the place of one. But there cannot be much spirit of self-government about us, if we take away or allow others to take away from them almost the whole of the results of their labour. Our salvation can only come through the farmer. Neither the lawyers, nor the doctors, nor the rich landlords are going to secure it.

Now, last but not the least, it is my bounden duty to refer to what agitated our minds during these two or three days. All of us have had many anxious moments while the Viceroy was going through the streets of Banaras. There were detectives stationed in many places. We were horrified. We asked ourselves, 'Why this distrust?'

Is it not better that even Lord Hardinge should die than live a living death? But a representative of a mighty sovereign may not. He might find it necessary to impose these detectives on us. We may foam, we may fret, we may resent, but let us not forget that India of today in her impatience has produced an army of anarchists. I myself am an anarchist, but of another type. But there is a class of anarchists amongst us, and if I was able to reach this class, I would say to them that their anarchism has no room in India, if India is to conquer the conqueror. It is a sign of fear. If we trust and fear God, we shall have to fear no one, not the Maharajas, not the Viceroys, not the detectives, not even King George.

I honour the anarchist for his love of the country. I honour him for his bravery in being willing to die for his country; but I ask him, is killing honourable? Is the dagger of an assassin a fit precursor of an honourable death? I deny it. There is no warrant for such methods in any scriptures. If I found it necessary for the salvation of India that the English should retire, that they should be driven out, I would not hesitate to declare that they would have to go, and I hope I would be prepared to die in defence of that belief. That would, in my opinion, be an honourable death. The bomb-thrower creates secret plots, is afraid to come out into the open, and when caught pays the penalty of misdirected zeal.

...I want to purge India of this atmosphere of suspicion on either side, if we are to reach our goal; we should have an empire which is to be based upon mutual love and mutual trust. Is it not better that we talk under the shadow of this college than that we should be talking irresponsibly in our homes? I consider that it is much better that we talk these things openly. I have done so with excellent results before now. I know that there is nothing that the students do not know. I am, therefore, turning the searchlight towards ourselves. I hold the name of my country so dear to me that I exchange these thoughts with you and submit to you that there is no room for anarchism in India. Let us frankly and openly say whatever we want to say to our rulers and face the consequences if what we have to say does not please them. But let us not abuse.

# BALGANGADHAR TILAK

## Freedom Is My Birthright

*Nashik, 1917*

*Balgangadhar Tilak (1856–1920), known as 'The Father of the Indian Unrest', was one of the first leaders of the Indian independence movement. He published two newspapers,* Kesari *and* The Mahratta, *in which he bitterly criticized the British government. He and Annie Besant founded the Home Rule League in 1916. Tilak delivered the following speech at Nashik in 1917, on the first anniversary of the formation of the Home Rule League.*

I am young in spirit though old in body. I do not wish to lose this privilege of youth. Whatever I am going to speak today is eternally young. The body might grow old, decrepit and it might perish, but the soul is immortal. Similarly, if there might be an apparent lull in our home rule activities, the freedom of the spirit behind it is eternal and indestructible, and it will secure liberty for us. Freedom is my birthright. So long as it is awake within me, I am not old. No weapon can cut this spirit, no fire can burn it, no water can wet it, no wind can dry it. We ask for home rule and we must get it. The science which ends in home rule is the science of politics and not the one which ends in slavery. The science of politics is the 'veda' of the country. You have a soul and I only want to awaken it. I want to tear off the blind that has been let down by ignorant, conniving and selfish people. The science of politics consists of two parts. The first is divine and the second is demonic. The slavery of a nation constitutes the latter. There cannot be a moral justification for the demonic part of the science of politics. A nation which might justify this, is guilty of sin in the sight of God. Some people do and some do not have the courage to declare what is harmful for them. Political and religious teaching consists in giving the knowledge of this principle.

Religious and political teachings are not separate, though they appear to be so on account of foreign rule. All philosophies are included in the science of politics.

Who does not know the meaning of home rule? Who does not want it? Would you like it if I enter your house and take possession of your kitchen? I must have the right to manage the affairs in my own house. We are told we are not fit for home rule. A century has passed and the British Rule has not made us fit for home rule; now we will make our own efforts and make ourselves fit for it. To offer irrelevant excuses, to hold out any temptations and to make other offers will be putting a stigma on English policy. England is trying to protect the small state of Belgium with India's help; how can it then say that we should not have home rule? Those who find fault with us are avaricious people. But there are people who find fault even with the all-merciful God. We must work hard to save the soul of our nation without caring for anything. The good of our country consists in guarding this birth right. The Congress has passed this home rule resolution.

In practical politics some futile objections are raised to oppose our desire for swaraj. Illiteracy of the bulk of our people is one of such objections; but to my mind it ought not to be allowed to stand in our way. It would be sufficient for us even if the illiterate in our country have only a vague conception of swaraj, just as it all goes well with them if they simply have a hazy idea about God. Those who can efficiently manage their own affairs may be illiterate; but they are not idiots. They are as intelligent as any other educated man and if they could understand their immediate concerns they would not find any difficulty in grasping the principle of swaraj. If illiteracy is not a disqualification in civil law there is no reason why it should not be so in nature's law also. Even the illiterate are our brethren: they have the same rights and are actuated by the same aspirations. It is, therefore, our bounden duty to awaken the masses. Circumstances have changed, and are favourable. The voice has gone forth 'Now or Never.' Rectitude and constitutional agitation is alone what is expected of you. Turn not back, and confidently leave the ultimate issue to the benevolence of the Almighty.

## RABINDRANATH TAGORE

### Crisis of Civilization

*Shantiniketan, 1941*

*Rabindranath Tagore (1861–1941) was a writer, poet, artist, musician and cultural reformer. Among the songs he wrote are the national anthems of two countries—India and Bangladesh. He also founded the Visva-Bharati University in Shantiniketan in 1901. Every year, around his birthday celebrations in the university in May, he would read out a message to his well-wishers. The following are excerpts from a speech he delivered on 7 May 1941, a day before his birthday, and that was to be the last speech he delivered before his death later that year. It is a classic example of his engagement with the world around him, particularly India under the British rule.*

Today I complete eighty years of my life. As I look back on the vast stretch of years that lie behind me and see in clear perspective the history of my early development, I am struck by the change that has taken place both in my own attitude and in the psychology of my countrymen—a change that carries within it a cause of profound tragedy.

Our direct contact with the larger world of men was linked up with the contemporary history of the English people whom we came to know in those earlier days. It was mainly through their mighty literature that we formed our ideas with regard to these newcomers to our Indian shores. In those days the type of learning that was served out to us was neither plentiful nor diverse, nor was the spirit of scientific enquiry very much in evidence. Thus their scope being strictly limited, the educated of those days had recourse to English language and literature. Their days and nights were eloquent with the stately declamations of Burke, with Macaulay's long-rolling sentences; discussions centred upon Shakespeare's drama and Byron's poetry and above all upon the large-hearted liberalism of the nineteenth-century English politics.

At the time though tentative attempts were being made to gain our national independence, at heart we had not lost faith in the generosity of the English race. This belief was so firmly rooted in the sentiments of our leaders as to lead them to hope that the victor would of his own grace pave the path of freedom for the vanquished. This belief was based upon the fact that England at the time provided shelter to all those who had to flee from persecution in their own country. Political martyrs who had suffered for the honour of their people were accorded unreserved welcome at the hands of the English.

I was impressed by this evidence of liberal humanity in the character of the English and thus I was led to set them on the pedestal of my highest respect. This generosity in their national character had not yet been vitiated by imperialist pride. About this time, as a boy in England, I had the opportunity of listening to the speeches of John Bright, both in and outside Parliament. The large-hearted, radical liberalism of those speeches, overflowing all narrow national bounds, had made so deep an impression on my mind that something of it lingers even today, even in these days of graceless disillusionment.

Certainly that spirit of abject dependence upon the charity of our rulers was no matter for pride. What was remarkable, however, was the wholehearted way in which we gave our recognition to human greatness even when it revealed itself in the foreigner. The best and noblest gifts of humanity cannot be the monopoly of a particular race or country; its scope may not be limited nor may it be regarded as the miser's hoard buried underground. That is why English literature which nourished our minds in the past, does even now convey its deep resonance to the recesses of our heart.

It is difficult to find a suitable Bengali equivalent for the English word 'civilization'. That phase of civilization with which we were familiar in this country has been called by Manu 'Sadachar' (literally, proper conduct), that is, the conduct prescribed by the tradition of the race.

Narrow in themselves, these time-honoured social conventions originated and held good in a circumscribed geographical area, in that strip of land, Brahmavarta by name, bound on either side by the rivers Saraswati and Drisadvati. That is how a pharisaic formalism gradually got the upper hand of free thought and the ideal of 'proper conduct' which Manu found established in Brahmavarta steadily degenerated into socialized tyranny. During my boyhood days the attitude towards the cultured and educated section of Bengal, nurtured on English learning, was charged with a feeling of revolt against these rigid regulations of society.

A perusal of what Rajnarain Bose has written describing the ways of the educated gentry of those days will amply bear out what I have said just now. In place of these set codes of conduct we accepted the ideal of 'civilization' as represented by the English term.

In our own family this change of spirit was welcomed for the sake of its sheer rational and moral force and its influence was felt in every sphere of our life. Born in that atmosphere, which was moreover coloured by our intuitive bias for literature, I naturally set the English on the throne of my heart. Thus passed the first chapters of my life. Then came the parting of ways accompanied with a painful feeling of disillusion when I began increasingly to discover how easily those who accepted the highest truths of civilization disowned them with impunity whenever questions of national self-interest were involved.

There came a time when perforce I had to snatch myself away from the mere appreciation of literature. As I emerged into the stark light of bare facts, the sight of the dire poverty of the Indian masses rent my heart. Rudely shaken out of my dreams, I began to realize that perhaps in no other modern state was there such hopeless dearth of the most elementary needs of existence. And yet it was this country whose resources had fed for so long the wealth and magnificence of the British people.

While I was lost in the contemplation of

the great world of civilization, I could never have remotely imagined that the great ideals of humanity would end in such ruthless travesty. But today a glaring example of it stares me in the face in the utter and contemptuous indifference of a so-called civilized race to the well being of crores of Indian people. That mastery over the machine, by which the British have consolidated their sovereignty over their vast Empire, has been kept a sealed book, to which due access has been denied to this helpless country....

When I see elsewhere some two hundred nationalities—which only a few years ago were at vastly different stages of development—marching ahead in peaceful progress and amity, and when I look about my own country and see a very highly evolved and intellectual people drifting into the disorder of barbarism, I cannot help contrasting the two systems of governments, one based on co-operation, the other on exploitation, which have made such contrary conditions possible.

... In India the misfortune of being governed

by a foreign race is daily brought home to us not only in the callous neglect of such minimum necessities of life as adequate provision for food, clothing, education and medical facilities for the people, but in an even unhappier form in the way people have divided themselves. The pity of it is that the blame is laid at the door of our own society. So frightful a culmination of the history of our people would never have been possible, but for the encouragement it has received from secret influences emanating from high places.

One cannot believe that Indians are in any way inferior to the Japanese in intellectual capacity. The most effective difference between these two eastern peoples is that whereas India lies at the mercy of the British, Japan has been spared the shadow of alien domination. We know what we have been deprived of. That which was truly best in their own civilizations, the upholding of the dignity of human relationships, has no place in the British administration of this country.

If in its place they have established, with

baton in hand, a reign of 'law and order', in other words a policeman's rule, such mockery of civilization can claim no respect from us. It is the mission of civilization to bring unity among people and establish peace and harmony. But in unfortunate India the social fabric is being rent into shreds by unseemly outbursts of hooliganism daily growing in intensity, right under the very aegis of 'law and order'.

In India, so long as no personal injury is inflicted upon any member of the ruling race, this barbarism seems to be assured of perpetuity, making us ashamed to live under such an administration.

## MAHATMA GANDHI

### Quit India

*Bombay, 1942*

*On 8 August 1942 in Bombay, Mahatma Gandhi delivered the following speech, which heralded the Quit India Movement. In this speech he called for a total commitment to Ahimsa (non-violence) in the Independence struggle.*

Before you discuss the resolution, let me place before you one or two things, I want you to understand two things very clearly and to consider them from the same point of view from which I am placing them before you. I ask you to consider it from my point of view, because if you approve of it, you will be enjoined to carry out all I say. It will be a great responsibility. There are people who ask me whether I am the same man that I was in 1920, or whether there has been any change in me. You are right in asking that question.

Let me, however, hasten to assure that I am the same Gandhi as I was in 1920. I have not changed in any fundamental respect. I attach the same importance to non-violence that I did then. If at all, my emphasis on it has grown stronger. There is no real contradiction between the present resolution and my previous writings and utterances.

Occasions like the present do not occur in everybody's and but rarely in anybody's life. I want you to know and feel that there is nothing but purest Ahimsa in all that I am saying and doing today. The draft resolution of the Working Committee is based on Ahimsa, the contemplated struggle similarly has its roots in Ahimsa. If, therefore, there is any among you who has lost faith in Ahimsa or is wearied of it, let him not vote for this resolution.

Let me explain my position clearly. God has vouchsafed to me a priceless gift in the weapon of Ahimsa. I and my Ahimsa are on our trail today. If in the present crisis, when the earth is being scorched by the flames of Himsa and crying for deliverance, I fail to make use of the God given talent, God will not forgive me and I shall be judged un-wrongly of the great gift. I must act now. I may not hesitate and merely look on, when Russia and China are threatened.

Ours is not a drive for power, but purely a non-violent fight for India's independence. In a violent struggle, a successful general has been often known to effect a military coup and to set up a dictatorship. But under the Congress scheme of things, essentially non-violent as it is, there can be no room for dictatorship. A non-violent soldier of freedom will covet nothing for himself; he fights only for the freedom of his country. The Congress is unconcerned as to who will rule, when freedom is attained. The power, when it comes, will belong to the people of India, and it will be for them to decide to whom it placed in the entrusted. May be that the reins will be placed in the hands of the Parsis, for instance—as I would love to see happen—or they may be handed to some others whose names are not heard in the Congress today. It will not be for you then to object saying, 'This community is microscopic. That party did not play its due part in the freedom's struggle; why should it have all the power?' Ever since its inception the Congress has kept itself meticulously free of the communal taint. It has thought always in terms of the whole nation and has acted accordingly...

I know how imperfect our Ahimsa is and how far away we are still from the ideal, but in Ahimsa there is no final failure or defeat. I have faith, therefore, that if, in spite of our shortcomings, the big thing does happen, it will be because God wanted to help us by crowning with success our silent, unremitting Sadhana for the last twenty-two years.

I believe that in the history of the world, there has not been a more genuinely democratic struggle for freedom than ours. I read Carlyle's *French Revolution* while I was in prison, and Pandit Jawaharlal has told me something about the Russian revolution. But it is my conviction that inasmuch as these struggles were fought with the weapon of violence they failed to realize the democratic ideal. In the democracy which I have envisaged, a democracy established by non-violence, there will be equal freedom for all. Everybody will be his own master. It is to join a struggle for such democracy that I invite you today. Once you realize this you will forget the differences between the Hindus and Muslims, and think of yourselves as Indians only, engaged in the common struggle for independence.

Then, there is the question of your attitude towards the British. I have noticed that there is hatred towards the British among the people. The people say they are disgusted with their behaviour. The people make no distinction between British imperialism and the British people. To them, the two are one. This hatred would even make them welcome the Japanese. It is most dangerous. It means that they will exchange one slavery for another. We must get rid of this feeling. Our quarrel is not with the

British people, we fight their imperialism. The proposal for the withdrawal of British power did not come out of anger. It came to enable India to play its due part at the present critical juncture. It is not a happy position for a big country like India to be merely helping with money and material obtained willy-nilly from her while the United Nations are conducting the war. We cannot evoke the true spirit of sacrifice and valour, so long as we are not free.

I know the British Government will not be able to withhold freedom from us, when we have made enough self-sacrifice. We must, therefore, purge ourselves of hatred. Speaking for myself, I can say that I have never felt any hatred. As a matter of fact, I feel myself to be a greater friend of the British now than ever before. One reason is that they are today in distress. My very friendship, therefore, demands that I should try to save them from their mistakes. As I view the situation, they are on the brink of an abyss. It, therefore, becomes my duty to warn them of their danger even though it may, for the time being, anger them to the point of cutting off the friendly hand that is stretched out to help them. People may laugh, nevertheless that is my claim. At a time when I may have to launch the biggest struggle of my life, I may not harbour hatred against anybody.

# SUBHASH CHANDRA BOSE

## Give Me Blood and I Promise You Freedom

*Burma, 1944*

*Subhash Chandra Bose (1897–1945?), also known as 'Netaji', set up and commanded the Indian National Army (INA) in order to liberate India from British rule. The following speech, delivered to the Indian National Army in Burma in 1944, is perhaps one of his most famous and inspirational speeches.*

Friends! Twelve months ago a new programme of 'total mobilization' or 'maximum sacrifice' was placed before Indians in East Asia. Today I shall give you an account of our achievements during the past year and shall place before you our demands for the coming year. But, before I do so, I want you to realize once again what a golden opportunity we have for winning freedom. The British are engaged in a worldwide struggle and in the course of this struggle they have suffered defeat after defeat on so many fronts. The enemy having been thus considerably weakened, our fight for liberty has become very much easier than it was five years ago. Such a rare and God-given opportunity comes once in a century. That is why we have sworn to fully utilize this opportunity for liberating our motherland from the British yoke.

I am so very hopeful and optimistic about the outcome of our struggle, because I do not rely merely on the efforts of three million Indians in East Asia. There is a gigantic movement going on inside India and millions of our countrymen are prepared for maximum suffering and sacrifice in order to achieve liberty.

Unfortunately, ever since the great fight of 1857, our countrymen are disarmed, whereas the enemy is armed to the teeth. Without arms and without a modern army, it is impossible for a disarmed people to win freedom in this modern age. Through the grace of Providence and through the help of generous Nippon, it has become possible for Indians in East Asia to get arms to build up a modern army. Moreover, Indians in East Asia are united to a man in the endeavour to win freedom, and all the religious and other differences that the British tried to engineer inside India, simply do not exist in East Asia.

Consequently, we have now an ideal combination of circumstances favouring the success of our struggle and all that is wanted is that Indians should themselves come forward to pay the price of liberty. According to the programme of 'total mobilization,' I demanded of you men, money and materials. Regarding men, I am glad to tell you that I have obtained sufficient recruits already. Recruits have come to us from every corner of East Asia—from China, Japan, Indo-China, Philippines, Java, Borneo, Celebes, Sumatra, Malaya, Thailand and Burma...

You must continue the mobilization of men, money and materials with greater vigour and energy, in particular, the problem of supplies and transport has to be solved satisfactorily.

We require more men and women of all categories for administration and reconstruction in liberated areas. We must be prepared for a situation in which the enemy will ruthlessly apply the scorched earth policy, before withdrawing from a particular area and will also force the civilian population to evacuate as was attempted in Burma.

Those of you who will continue to work on the Home Front should never forget that East Asia—and particularly Burma—form our base for the war of liberation. If this base is not strong, our fighting forces can never be victorious. Remember that this is a 'total war'—and not merely a war between two armies. That is why for a full one year I have been laying so much stress on 'total mobilization' in the East.

There is another reason why I want you to look after the Home Front properly. During the coming months I and my colleagues on the War Committee of the Cabinet desire to devote our whole attention to the fighting front and also to the task of working up the revolution inside India. Consequently, we want to be fully assured that the work at the base will go on smoothly and uninterruptedly even in our absence.

Friends, one year ago, when I made certain demands of you, I told you that if you give me 'total mobilization,' I would give you a 'second front.' I have redeemed that pledge. The first phase of our campaign is over. Our victorious troops, fighting side by side with Nipponese troops, have pushed back the enemy and are now fighting bravely on the sacred soil of our dear motherland.

Gird up your loins for the task that now lies ahead. I had asked you for men, money and materials. I have got them in generous measure. Now I demand more of you. Men, money and materials cannot by themselves bring victory or freedom. We must have the motive-power that will inspire us to brave deeds and heroic exploits.

It will be a fatal mistake for you to wish to live and see India free simply because victory is now within reach. No one here should have the desire to live to enjoy freedom. A long fight is still in front of us.

We should have but one desire today—the desire to die so that India may live—the desire to face a martyr's death, so that the path to freedom may be paved with the martyr's blood.

Friends! My comrades in the War of Liberation! Today I demand of you one thing, above all. I demand of you blood. It is blood alone that can avenge the blood that the enemy has spilt. It is blood alone that can pay the price of freedom. Give me blood and I promise you freedom.

## S. RADHAKRISHNAN

The Spirit of India

*Delhi, 1946*

*Dr Sarvepalli Radhakrishnan (1888–1975) served as India's first Vice President and second President. As a scholar, he published important works that brought Indian philosophy to a global audience. He was much loved by his students throughout his career, and his birthday, 5 September, is celebrated as Teacher's Day. Following is the speech he delivered at the Constituent Assembly on 11 December 1946. In this speech, he highlighted the need for a fair and just Indian Constitution.*

Mr President, Sir, I consider it a great honour to be called upon to be the first speaker after the election of the permanent Chairman of the Constituent Assembly. I offer to him, on behalf of this House, our most respectful congratulations on the unique honour that has been conferred on him. This Constituent Assembly has met here to frame the constitution, to effect the withdrawal of British control—political, economic and military—and to establish a free independent India. If successful, this transfer of authority will be the biggest and the least bloody of all transfers in human history. [Cheers]

The first Britisher to arrive in this country was a Jesuit Missionary in 1579. He was followed by merchants who came to trade but stayed to rule. In 1765 the authority was transferred to the East India Company. Later, it was gradually subordinated to and replaced by the authority of Parliament and it has been continuing till now on the famous principle enunciated by Cecil Rhodes—the principle fundamental to imperialism, philanthropy plus 5 per cent. On that principle it has worked. Right through however there were protests against the British rule. All these protests became canalized when the Indian National Congress was established in 1885. It adopted mild methods till the advent of Mahatma Gandhi when it became aggressive and dynamic. In 1930 the Resolution for the Independence of India was passed at Lahore and we are now here to give effect to that resolution.

The British are empirics from beginning to end. It was Lord Palmerston who said 'we British have no eternal principles, we have only eternal interests.' When they adopt any particular line of action you 'May take it that it is not a willing surrender of power or authority but it is response to the historic necessities of the case.' When the discontent grew they gave us the Morley–Minto Reforms and they introduced the principle of communal electorates and these communal electorates were intended to keep the people apart, the higher mind of Britain advised the local officials that they would betray the trust placed upon them if they foisted communal electorates. They would inject a poison into the very body politic which could be removed if at all, at the cost of a civil war. We know how those anticipations are getting realized today.

We had after that the Montford Reforms and then the 1935 Act, the Cripps' proposals and now the Cabinet Plan. The latest statement of His Majesty's Government on this question indicates how it is not in human nature to surrender power easily. [Hear, hear] Playing off one section against another is unworthy of a great people. It is much too clever to be permanent and would embitter the relations of this country and Great Britain. [Hear, hear] It is essential for the British to understand that if an act is done it must be done with the utmost grace.

We are here assembled to draw up a constitution for future India. A constitution is the fundamental law of the nation. It should embody and express the dreams and passions, the ideals and aspirations of the people. It must be based on the consent of all, and respect the rights of all people who belong to this great land. We have been kept apart. It is our duty now to find each other. We all deplore—speakers yesterday and day before yesterday deplored—the abstention of the representatives of the Muslim League from this Constituent Assembly. We take it that it will only be temporary, for their cooperation is absolutely essential for the success of any constitution which we may lay down. But in approaching these matters our attitude should be one of realism. Take the problems from which we suffer: our hunger, our poverty, our disease, our malnutrition—these are common to all. Take the psychological evils from which we suffer—the loss of human dignity, the slavery of the mind, the stunting of sensibility and the shame of subjection. These are common to all: Hindus or Muslims, Princes or peasants. The chains may be made of gold but they are still chains that fetter us. Even the Princes will have to realize that they are slaves in this country. [Hear, hear] If they have a sufficient sense of self-respect and exercise a little self-analysis, they will find how much their freedom is fettered. Again, the, people, whether they are Hindus or Muslims, Princes or peasants, belong to this one country. Earth and Heaven have combined to make them belong to one another. If they try to disown it, their gait, their cast of countenance, their modes of thought, their ways of behaviour, they will all betray them. [Hear, hear] It is not possible for us to think that we belong to different nationalities. Our whole ancestry is there.

It is essential for any constitution which is drawn up to make all the citizens realize that their basic privileges—education, social and economic—are afforded to them; that there will be cultural autonomy; that nobody will be suppressed; that it will be a constitution which will be democratic in the true sense of the term, where, from political freedom we will march on to economic freedom and equity. Every individual should feel that he is proud to belong to this great land. Apart from all these, a nation does not depend on identity of race, or sentiment, or on ancestral memories, but it depends on a persistent and continuous way of life that has come down to us. Such a way of life belongs to the very soil of this land. It is indigenous to this country as much as the waters of the Ganges or the snows of the Himalayas.

From the very roots of our civilization down in the Indus Valley to the present day, the same great culture is represented among Hindus and Muslims, we have stood for the ideal of comprehension and charity all these centuries.

...India is a symphony where there are, as in an orchestra, different instruments, each with its particular sonority, each with its special sound, all combining to interpret one particular score. It is this kind of combination that this country has stood for. It never adopted inquisitorial methods. It never asked the Parsis or the Jews or the Christians or the Muslims who came and took shelter here to change their creeds or become absorbed in what might be called a uniform Hindu humanity. It never did this. 'Live and let live'—that has been the spirit of this country. If we are true to that spirit, if that ideal which has dominated our cultural landscape for five or six thousand years and is still operating, I have no doubt that the crisis by which we are faced today will be overcome as many other crises in our previous history have been overcome.

## RAJENDRA PRASAD

On the Constituent Assembly

*Delhi, 1946*

*Dr Rajendra Prasad (1884–1963), the first President of the Republic of India, was a prominent activist of the Indian Independence movement. Following is the speech he delivered at the Constituent Assembly on 11 December 1946, after being elected as its permanent chairman. In this significant speech, he set an agenda for the workings of the Constituent Assembly.*

I am aware that my path is beset with obstacles. The work of this Constituent Assembly is most arduous. Various problems will come before it and it will be confronted with questions which will not yield easily to solution. I know I will not be able to solve them but I have full confidence in you that you will help me at each step with the same kindness and liberality with which you have elected me here.

The Constituent Assembly is meeting at a most critical time. We all know that other constituent assemblies, whenever and wherever they met, were confronted with similar difficulties. They had also to contend with internal differences which were placed before them with great vehemence. We also know that many of these constituent assemblies were held amidst strife and bloodshed; even their proceedings were conducted amidst quarrels and fights. In spite of all these obstacles those assemblies carried on their work to the end. Their members joined together and with courage, kindness, generosity, tolerance and regard for one another's feelings framed constitutions which were then readily accepted by the people of the countries for which they were framed. Even at this time the people of those countries consider them their most valuable possession. There is no reason why our Constituent Assembly, in spite of the obstructions in its way, should not succeed in doing its work. If we are sincere, if we respect each other's opinion, we shall develop so much insight that we will not only be able to understand each other's thoughts, but also be able to go deep to the root and understand each other's real troubles. We will then function in a manner that will give no one cause to think that he has been ignored or that his opinion has not been respected. If this comes to pass and if this strength is born in us, I have full faith that in spite of all obstruction we will succeed in our work.

This Constituent Assembly has come into being despite a number of limitations, many of which we will have to bear in mind as we proceed. But, it must also be borne in mind that the Assembly is a sovereign body and is fully competent to conduct its proceedings in the manner it chooses to follow. No outside power can meddle with its proceedings. I also believe that it is competent to break the limitations attached to it at its birth. It should be our effort to get free of these limitations and frame a constitution which will assure all men and women of this country, no matter of what religion, province or shade of opinion, that their rights are fully protected. If such an effort is made in this House and we succeed in it, I believe that it will be such a landmark in the history of the world that it will be hard to rival. It is also to be remembered and we, who are present in the House, cannot forget it even for a moment that many of the seats are vacant in this meeting. Our brethren of the Muslim League are not with us and their absence increases our responsibility. We shall have to think at each step what would they have done if they were here? We have to proceed keeping all these things in view. We hope they will soon come and take their places and share in the deliberations for framing a constitution for their country which will give it freedom, that they will join us in our march for freedom. But if unfortunately these seats continue to remain unoccupied, it will be our duty to frame a constitution which will leave no room for complaint from anybody.

We have been fighting for the freedom of our country for a long time. This Constituent Assembly has been brought into existence by three forces. First, the sacrifice of our patriots. Many men and women gave their lives, bore hardships and persecution and after hard and continuous struggles ushered in the present stage. Second, the history of the British nation; their selfishness and their generosity. Third, the present world conditions and serious situation and the forces that are raging in the world. All these combined together to bring into being our Constituent Assembly. These forces will continue functioning while we are proceeding with our work. It is quite possible that some of them may draw us to one side and others to the other side. I am, however, confident that success will be ours. I pray to God that he may give us foresight, so that we may understand each other's mind, and that, united together, we may free our country.

# JAIPAL SINGH MUNDA

## On Representation of the Minorities

*Delhi, 1946*

*Jaipal Singh Munda (1903–1970), popularly known as Marang Gomke, represented the Adivasis of India at the Constituent Assembly. During this time, he actively championed the rights of the Scheduled Tribes. Following are excerpts from the first speech he made at the Constituent Assembly on 16 December 1946.*

Mr Chairman, Sir, I rise to speak on behalf of millions of unknown hordes—yet very important—of unrecognized warriors of freedom, the original people of India who have variously been known as backward tribes, primitive tribes, criminal tribes and everything else. Sir, I am proud to be a Jungli, that is the name by which we are known in my part of the country. Living as we do in the jungles, we know what it means to support this Resolution. On behalf of more than thirty million of the Adibasis [cheers], I support it not merely because it may have been sponsored by a leader of the Indian National Congress. I support it because it is a resolution which gives expression to sentiments that throb in every heart in this country. I have no quarrel with the wording of this Resolution at all. As a jungli, as an Adibasi, I am not expected to understand the legal intricacies of the Resolution. But my common sense tells me, the common sense of my people tells me that every one of us should march in that road of freedom and fight together. Sir, if there is any group of Indian people that has been shabbily treated it is my people. They have been disgracefully treated, neglected for the last 6,000 years. The history of the Indus Valley civilization, a child of which I am, shows quite clearly that it is the newcomers—most of you here are intruders as far as I am concerned—

who have driven away my people from the Indus Valley to the jungle fastness. This Resolution is not going to teach Adibasis democracy. You cannot teach democracy to the tribal people; you have to learn democratic ways from them. They are the most democratic people on earth. What my people require, Sir, is not adequate safeguards as Pandit Jawaharlal Nehru has put it. They require protection from Ministers, that is position today. We do not ask for any special protection. We want to be treated like every other Indian.

There is the problem of Hindustan. There is position of Pakistan. There is the problem of Adibasis. If we all shout in different militant directions, feel in different ways, we shall end up in Kabarasthan. The whole history of my people is one of continuous exploitation and dispossession by the non-aboriginals of India punctuated by rebellions and disorder, and yet I take Pandit Jawaharlal Nehru at his word. I take you all at your word that now we are going to start a new chapter, a new chapter of

Independent India where there is equality of opportunity, where no one would be neglected. There is no question of caste in my society. We are all equal....

I have heard of resolutions and speeches galore assuring Adibasis of a fair deal. If history had to teach me anything at all, I should distrust this Resolution, but I do not. Now we are on a new road. Now we have simply got to learn to trust each other. And I ask friends who are not present with us today that they should come in, they should trust us and we, in turn, must learn to trust them. We must create a new atmosphere of confidence among ourselves.

## JAWAHARLAL NEHRU

### A Tryst with Destiny

*Delhi, 1947*

*A major figure of the Indian Independence movement, Jawaharlal Nehru (1889–1964) was the first Prime Minister of independent India. He was a charismatic leader and was respected all around the world. On the midnight of 14 August 1947, Nehru delivered the following speech, announcing the dawn of an independent India to the world.*

Long years ago we made a tryst with destiny, and now the time comes when we shall redeem our pledge, not wholly or in full measure, but very substantially. At the stroke of the midnight hour, when the world sleeps, India will awake to life and freedom. A moment comes, which comes but rarely in history, when we step out from the old to the new, when an age ends, and when the soul of a nation, long suppressed, finds utterance. It is fitting that at this solemn moment, we take the pledge of dedication to the service of India and her people and to the still larger cause of humanity.

At the dawn of history, India started on her unending quest, and trackless centuries are filled with her striving and grandeur of her success and failures. Through good and ill fortune alike, she has never lost sight of that quest or forgotten the ideals which gave her strength. We end today a period of misfortunes and India discovers herself again. The achievement we celebrate today is but a step, an opening of opportunity to the greater triumphs and achievements that await us. Are we brave enough and wise enough to grasp this opportunity and accept the challenge of the future?

Freedom and power bring responsibility. The responsibility rests upon this Assembly, a sovereign body representing the sovereign people of India. Before the birth of freedom, we have endured all the pains of labour and our hearts are heavy with the memory of this sorrow. Some of those pains continue even now. Nevertheless, the past is over and it is the future that beckons us now.

That future is not one of ease or resting but of incessant striving so that we may fulfill the pledges we have so often taken and the one we shall take today. The service of India means the service of the millions who suffer. It means the ending of poverty and ignorance and disease and inequality of opportunity. The ambition of the greatest man of our generation has been to wipe every tear from every eye. That may be beyond us, but as long as there are tears and suffering, so long our work will not be over.

And so we have to labour and to work, and to work hard, to give reality to our dreams. Those dreams are for India, but they are also for the world, for all the nations and peoples are too closely knit together today for any one of them to imagine that it can live apart. Peace is said to be indivisible, so is freedom, so is prosperity now, and also is disaster in this one world that can no longer be split into isolated fragments.

## JAWAHARLAL NEHRU

### The Light Has Gone Out of Our Lives

*Delhi, 1948*

*Mahatma Gandhi's assassination on 30 January 1948 plunged the entire country and indeed the world into shock. Jawaharlal Nehru spoke these heartfelt words while addressing the country and informing about the death of Bapu. It was broadcast on All India Radio on the same day.*

Friends and Comrades,
The light has gone out of our lives and there is darkness everywhere. I do not know what to tell you and how to say it. Our beloved leader, Bapu as we called him, the Father of the Nation, is no more. Perhaps I am wrong to say that. Nevertheless, we will never see him again as we have seen him for these many years. We will not

run to him for advice and seek solace from him, and that is a terrible blow, not to me only, but to millions and millions in this country. And it is a little difficult to soften the blow by any other advice that I or anyone else can give you.

The light has gone out, I said, and yet I was wrong. For the light that shone in this country was no ordinary light. The light that has illumined this country for these many years will illumine this country for many more years, and a thousand years later, that light will be seen in this country and the world will see it and it will give solace to innumerable hearts. For that light represented something more than the immediate past, it represented the living, the eternal truths, reminding us of the right path, drawing us from error, taking this ancient country to freedom.

All this has happened when there was so much more for him to do. We could never think that he was unnecessary or that he had done his task. But now, particularly, when we are faced with so many difficulties, his not being with us is a blow most terrible to bear.

A madman has put an end to his life, for I can only call him mad who did it, and yet there has been enough of poison spread in this country during the past years and months, and this poison has had an effect on people's minds. We must face this poison, we must root out this poison, and we must face all the perils that encompass us, and face them not madly or badly, but rather in the way that our beloved teacher taught us to face them.

The first thing to remember now is that none of us dare misbehave because he is angry. We have to behave like strong and determined people, determined to face all the perils that surround us, determined to carry out the mandate that our great teacher and our great leader has given us, remembering always that if, as I believe, his spirit looks upon us and sees us, nothing would displease his soul so much as to see that we have indulged in any small behaviour or any violence.

So we must not do that. But that does not mean that we should be weak, but rather that we should, in strength and in unity, face all the troubles that are in front of us. We must hold together, and all our petty troubles and difficulties and conflicts must be ended in the face of this great disaster. A great disaster is a symbol to us to remember all the big things of life and forget the small things of which we have thought too much. In his death he has reminded us of the big things of life, the living truth, and if we remember that, then it will be well with India...

It was proposed by some friends that Mahatmaji's body should be embalmed for a few days to enable millions of people to pay their last homage to him. But it was his wish, repeatedly expressed, that no such thing should happen, that this should not be done, that he was entirely opposed to any embalming of his body, and so we decided that we must follow his wishes in this matter, however much others might have wished otherwise.

And so the cremation will take place on Saturday in Delhi city by the side of the Jamuna

River. On Saturday forenoon, about 11.30 a.m., the bier will be taken out at Birla House and it will follow a prescribed road and go to the Jamuna River. The cremation will take place there at about 4 p.m. The place and the route will be announced by radio and the Press.

People in Delhi who wish to pay their last homage should gather along this route. I will not advise too many of them to come to Birla House, but rather to gather on both sides of this long route from Birla House to the Jamuna River. And I trust that they will remain there in silence without any demonstrations. That is the best way and the most fitting way to pay homage to this great soul. Also, Saturday should be a day of fasting and prayer for all of us.

Those who live elsewhere, out of Delhi and in other parts of India, will no doubt take such part as they can in this last homage. For them also, let this be a day of fasting and prayer. And at the appointed time for cremation, that is 4 p.m. on Saturday afternoon, people should go to the river or to the sea and offer prayers there.

And while we pray, the greatest prayer that we can offer is to take a pledge to dedicate ourselves to the truth, and to the cause for which this great countryman of ours lived and for which he has died. That is the best prayer that we can offer him and his memory. That is the best prayer we can offer to India and ourselves. Jai Hind.

## B.R. AMBEDKAR

### On the Threats to Democracy and the Constitution

*Delhi, 1949*

*Bhimrao Ramji Ambedkar (1891–1956) was one of the most important leaders and thinkers of modern India. He was also the chief architect of the Indian Constitution. Following is the speech he delivered at the Constituent Assembly Debate on 25 November 1949. In this extremely insightful speech, he warned his fellow members about the various possible threats to democracy in India.*

On the 26th of January 1950, India would be a democratic country in the sense that India from that day would have a government of the people, by the people and for the people. The same thought comes to my mind. What would happen to her democratic Constitution? Will she be able to maintain it or will she lose it again. This is the second thought that comes to my mind and makes me as anxious as the first.

It is not that India did not know what is Democracy. There was a time when India was studded with republics, and even where there were monarchies, they were either elected or limited. They were never absolute. It is not that India did not know Parliaments or Parliamentary Procedure. A study of the Buddhist Bhikshu Sanghas discloses that not only there were Parliaments—for the Sanghas were nothing but Parliaments—but the Sanghas knew and observed all the rules of Parliamentary Procedure known to modern times. They had rules regarding seating arrangements, rules regarding Motions, Resolutions, Quorum, Whip, Counting of Votes, Voting by Ballot, Censure Motion, Regularization, Res Judicata, etc. Although these rules of Parliamentary Procedure were applied by the Buddha to the meetings of the Sanghas, he must have borrowed them from the rules of the Political Assemblies functioning in the country in his time.

This democratic system India lost. Will she lose it a second time? I do not know. But it is quite possible in a country like India—where democracy from its long disuse must be regarded as something quite new—there is danger of democracy giving place to dictatorship. It is quite possible for this new-born democracy to retain its form but give place to dictatorship in fact. If there is a landslide, the danger of the second possibility becoming actuality is much greater.

If we wish to maintain democracy not merely in form, but also in fact, what must we do? The first thing in my judgement we must do is to hold fast to constitutional methods of achieving our social and economic objectives. It means we must abandon the bloody methods of revolution. It means that we must abandon the method of civil disobedience, non-cooperation and satyagraha. When there was no way left for constitutional methods for achieving economic and social objectives, there was a great deal of justification for unconstitutional methods. But where constitutional methods are open, there can be no justification for these unconstitutional methods. These methods are nothing but the Grammar of Anarchy and the sooner they are abandoned, the better for us.

The second thing we must do is to observe the caution which John Stuart Mill has given to all who are interested in the maintenance of democracy, namely, not 'to lay their liberties at the feet of even a great man, or to trust him with power which enable him to subvert their institutions'. There is nothing wrong in being grateful to great men who have rendered lifelong services to the country. But there are limits to gratefulness. As has been well said by the Irish Patriot Daniel O'Connel, no man can be grateful at the cost of his honour, no woman can be grateful at the cost of her chastity and no nation can be grateful at the cost of its liberty. This caution is far more necessary in the case of India than in the case of any other country. For in India, Bhakti or what may be called the path of devotion or hero-worship, plays a part in its politics unequalled in magnitude by the part it plays in the politics of any other country in the world. Bhakti in religion may be a road to the salvation of the soul. But in politics, Bhakti or hero-worship is a sure road to degradation and to eventual dictatorship.

The third thing we must do is not to be content with mere political democracy. We must make our political democracy a social democracy as well. Political democracy cannot last unless there lies at the base of it social democracy. What does social democracy mean? It means a way of life which recognizes liberty, equality and fraternity as the principles of life. These principles of liberty, equality and fraternity are not to be treated as separate items in a trinity. They form a union of trinity in the sense that to divorce one from the other is to defeat the very purpose of democracy. Liberty cannot be divorced from equality, equality cannot be divorced from liberty. Nor can liberty and equality be divorced from fraternity. Without equality, liberty would produce the supremacy of the few over the many. Equality without liberty would kill individual initiative. Without fraternity, liberty would produce the supremacy of the few over the many. Without fraternity, liberty and equality could not become a natural course of things. It would require a constable to enforce them. We must begin by acknowledging the fact that there is complete absence of two things in Indian society. One of these is equality. On the social plane, we have in India a society based on the principle of graded inequality which we have a society in which there are some who have immense wealth as against many who live in abject poverty.

On the 26th of January 1950, we are going to enter into a life of contradictions. In politics we will have equality and in social and economic life we will have inequality. In politics we will be recognizing the principle of one man one vote and one vote and one value. In our social and economic life, we shall, by reason of our social and economic structure, continue to deny the principle of one man one value. How long shall we continue to live this life of contradictions? How long shall we continue to deny equality in our social and economic life? If we continue to deny it for long, we will do so only by putting our political democracy in peril. We must remove this contradiction at the earliest possible moment or else those who suffer from inequality will blow up the structure of political democracy which this Assembly has laboriously built up.

The second thing we are wanting in is recognition of the principle of fraternity. What does fraternity mean? Fraternity means a sense of common brotherhood of all Indians—if Indians being one people. It is the principle which gives unity and solidarity to social life. It is a difficult thing to achieve. How difficult it is, can be realized from the story related by James Bryce in his volume on American Commonwealth about the United States of America.

The story is—I propose to recount it in the words of Bryce himself—that:

Some years ago the American Protestant Episcopal Church was occupied at its triennial Convention in revising its liturgy. It was thought desirable to introduce among the short sentence prayers a prayer for the whole people, and an eminent New England divine proposed the words `O Lord, bless our nation'. Accepted one afternoon, on the spur of the moment, the sentence was brought up next day for reconsideration, when so many objections were raised by the laity to the word 'nation' as importing too definite a recognition of national unity, that it was dropped, and instead there were adopted the words `O Lord, bless these United States.'

There was so little solidarity in the U.S.A. at the time when this incident occurred that the people of America did not think that they were a nation. If the people of the United States could not feel that they were a nation, how difficult it is for Indians to think that they are a nation. I remember the days when politically minded Indians, resented the expression 'the people of

India'. They preferred the expression 'the Indian nation'. I am of opinion that in believing that we are a nation, we are cherishing a great delusion. How can people divided into several thousands of castes be a nation? The sooner we realize that we are not as yet a nation in the social and psychological sense of the world, the better for us. For then only we shall realize the necessity of becoming a nation and seriously think of ways and means of realizing the goal. The realization of this goal is going to be very difficult—far more difficult than it has been in the United States. The United States has no caste problem. In India there are castes. The castes are anti-national. In the first place because they bring about separation in social life. They are anti-national also because they generate jealousy and antipathy between caste and caste. But we must overcome all these difficulties if we wish to become a nation in reality. For fraternity can be a fact only when there is a nation. Without fraternity equality and liberty will be no deeper than coats of paint.

These are my reflections about the tasks that lie ahead of us. They may not be very pleasant to some. But there can be no gainsaying that political power in this country has too long been the monopoly of a few and that many are not only beasts of burden, but also beasts of prey. This monopoly has not merely deprived them of their chance of betterment, it has sapped them of what may be called the significance of life. These down-trodden classes are tired of being governed. They are impatient to govern themselves. This urge for self-realization in the down-trodden classes must not be allowed to devolve into a class struggle or class war. It would lead to a division of the House. That would indeed be a day of disaster. For, as has been well said by Abraham Lincoln, a House divided against itself cannot stand very long. Therefore the sooner room is made for the realization of their aspiration, the better for the few, the better for the country, the better for the maintenance of its independence and the better for the continuance of its democratic structure.

This can only be done by the establishment of equality and fraternity in all spheres of life. That is why I have laid so much stress on them.

I do not wish to weary the House any further. Independence is no doubt a matter of joy. But let us not forget that this independence has thrown on us great responsibilities. By independence, we have lost the excuse of blaming the British for anything going wrong. If hereafter things go wrong, we will have nobody to blame except ourselves. There is great danger of things going wrong. Times are fast changing. People, including our own, are being moved by new ideologies. They are getting tired of Government by the people. They are prepared to have Governments for the people and are indifferent whether it is Government of the people and by the people. If we wish to preserve the Constitution in which we have sought to enshrine the principle of Government of the people, for the people and by the people, let us resolve not to be tardy in the recognition of the evils that lie across our path and which induce people to prefer Government for the people to Government by the people, nor to be weak in our initiative to remove them. That is the only way to serve the country. I know of no better.

## MOTHER TERESA

### Give Till It Hurts

*Oslo, 1979*

*Mother Teresa (1910–1997) was born Agnes Gonxhe Bojaxhiu in Albania. In 1950, she founded the Missionaries of Charity headquartered in Kolkata. The Missionaries of Charity runs homes for the dying, homeless and sick, as well as orphanages, schools and more. Mother Teresa was awarded the Nobel Peace Prize and on 11 December 1979 she delivered the following speech while accepting the award. In the speech, she spoke about her lifelong mission to help others and how everyone has something to give. Here are some excerpts.*

Let us thank God for the opportunity that we all have together today, for this gift of peace that reminds us that we have been created to live that peace.

It is not enough for us to say: I love God, but I do not love my neighbour. How can you love God whom you do not see, if you do not love your neighbor whom you see, whom you touch, with whom you live? And so this is very important for us to realise that love, to be true, has to hurt.

I never forget an opportunity I had in visiting a home where they had all these old parents of sons and daughters who had just put them in an institution and forgotten maybe. And I went there, and I saw in that home they had everything, beautiful things, but everybody was looking towards the door. And I did not see a single one with their smile on their face. And I turned to the Sister and I asked: How is it that the people they have everything here, why are they all looking towards the door, why are they not smiling? I am so used to see the smile on our people, even the dying one smile, and she said: This is nearly every day, they are expecting, they are hoping that a son or daughter will come to visit them. They are hurt because they are forgotten, and see—this is where love comes.

I was surprised in the West to see so many young boys and girls given into drugs, and I tried to find out why—why it is like that, and the answer was: Because there is no one in the family to receive them. Father and mother are so busy they have no time. We are talking of peace. These are things that break peace. Many people are very, very concerned with the children in India, with the children in Africa where quite a number die, maybe of malnutrition, of hunger and so on, but millions are dying deliberately by the will of the mother. And this is what is the greatest destroyer of peace today. And this I appeal in India, I appeal everywhere: Let us bring the child back, and this year being the child's year: What have we done for the child.

The poor people are very great people. They can teach us so many beautiful things. The other day one of them came to thank and said: You people who have vowed chastity you are the best people to teach us family planning. Because it is nothing more than self-control out of love for each other. And I think they said a beautiful sentence. And these are people who maybe have nothing to eat, maybe they have not a home where to live, but they are great people. The poor are very wonderful people. One evening we went out and we picked up four people from the street. And one of them was in a most terrible condition—and I told the Sisters: You take care of the other three, I will take care of this one that looked worse. So I did for her all that my love can do. I put her in bed, and there was such a beautiful smile on her face. She took hold of my hand, as she said one word only: Thank you—and she died.

I could not help but examine my conscience before her, and I asked what would I say if I was in her place. And my answer was very simple. I would have tried to draw a little attention to myself, I would have said I am hungry, that I am dying, I am cold, I am in pain, or something, but she gave me much more—she gave me her grateful love. And she died with a smile on her face. As that man whom we picked up from the drain, half eaten with worms, and we brought him to the home. I have lived like an animal in the street, but I am going to die like an angel, loved and cared for. And it was so wonderful to see the greatness of that man who could speak like that, who could die like that without blaming anybody, without cursing anybody, without comparing anything.

I believe that we are not real social workers. We may be doing social work in the eyes of the people, but we are really contemplatives in the heart of the world. And I think that we in our family don't need bombs and guns, to destroy to bring peace—just get together, love one another, bring that peace, that joy, that strength of presence of each other in the home. And we will be able to overcome all the evil that is in the world.

There is so much suffering, so much hatred, so much misery, and we with our prayer, with our sacrifice are beginning at home. Love begins at home, and it is not how much we do, but how much love we put in the action that we do.

Some time ago in Calcutta we had great

difficulty in getting sugar, and I don't know how the word got around to the children, and a little boy of four years old, Hindu boy, went home and told his parents: I will not eat sugar for three days, I will give my sugar to Mother Teresa for her children. After three days his father and mother brought him to our home. I had never met them before, and this little one could scarcely pronounce my name, but he knew exactly what he had come to do. He knew that he wanted to share his love.

And that is why I have received such a lot of love from you all. From the time that I have come here I have simply been surrounded with love.

And so here I am talking with you—I want you to find the poor here, right in your own home first. And begin love there. Be that good news to your own people. And find out about your next-door-neighbour—do you know who they are? I had the most extraordinary experience with a Hindu family who had eight children. A gentleman came to our house and said: Mother Teresa, there is a family with eight children, they had not eaten for so long—do something. So I took some rice and I went there immediately. And I saw the children—their eyes shining with hunger. I don't know if you have ever seen hunger, but I have seen it very often. And she took the rice, she divided the rice, and she went out. When she came back I asked her—where did you go, what did you do? And she gave me a very simple answer: They (her neighbours) are hungry also. What struck me most was that she knew—and who are they, a Muslim family—and she knew. I didn't bring more rice that evening because I wanted them to enjoy the joy of sharing. But there were those children, radiating joy, sharing the joy with their mother because she had the love to give. And you see this is where love begins—at home.

And I know well that you have not given from your abundance, but you have given until it has hurt you. And with this prize that I have received as a prize of peace, I am going to try to make the home for many people that have no home.

Because I believe that love begins at home, and if we can create a home for the poor—I think that more and more love will spread. And we will be able through this understanding love to bring peace, be good news to the poor.

To be able to do this, our Sisters, our lives have to be woven with prayer. They have to be woven with Christ to be able to understand, to be able to share. Because today there is so much suffering. Are we there to share that passion, to share that suffering of people. Around the world, not only in the poor countries, but I found the poverty of the West so much more difficult to remove. When I pick up a person from the street, hungry, I give him a plate of rice, a piece of bread, I have satisfied. I have removed that hunger. But a person that is shut out, that feels unwanted, unloved, terrified, the person that has been thrown out from society—that poverty is so hurtable and so much, and I find that very difficult. Our Sisters are working amongst that kind of people in the West. So you must pray for us that we may be able to be that good news, but we cannot do that without you, you have to do that here in your country.

How difficult we find it sometimes to smile at each other, and that the smile is the beginning of love. And so let us always meet each other with a smile, for the smile is the beginning of love, and once we begin to love each other naturally we want to do something.

The other day I received 15 dollars from a man who has been on his back for twenty years, and the only part that he can move is his right hand. And the only companion that he enjoys is smoking. And he said to me: I do not smoke for one week, and I send you this money. It must have been a terrible sacrifice for him, but see how beautiful, how he shared, and with that money I bought bread and I gave to those who are hungry with a joy on both sides, he was giving and the poor were receiving. This is something that you and I—it is a gift of God to us to be able to share our love with others. And let it be as it was for Jesus. Let us love one another as he loved us. Let us love Him with undivided love.

And the joy of loving Him and each other—let us give now—that Christmas is coming so close. Let us keep that joy of loving Jesus in our hearts. And share that joy with all that we come in touch with. And that radiating joy is real, for we have no reason not to be happy because we have no Christ with us. Christ in our hearts, Christ in the poor that we meet, Christ in the smile that we give and the smile that we receive. Let us make that one point: That no child will be unwanted, and also that we meet each other always with a smile, especially when it is difficult to smile.

I never forget some time ago about fourteen professors came from the United States from different universities. And they came to Calcutta to our house. Then we were talking about that they had been to the home for the dying. We have a home for the dying in Calcutta, where we have picked up more than 36,000 people only from the streets of Calcutta, and out of that big number more than 18,000 have died a beautiful death. They have just gone home to God; and they came to our house and we talked of love, of compassion, and then one of them asked me: Say, Mother, please tell us something that we will remember, and I said to them: Smile at each other, make time for each other in your family. Smile at each other. And then another one asked me: Are you married, and I said: Yes, and I find it sometimes very difficult to smile at Jesus because he can be very demanding sometimes. This is really something true, and there is where love comes—when it is demanding, and yet we can give it to Him with joy. Just as I have said today, I have said that if I don't go to Heaven for anything else I will be going to Heaven for all the publicity because it has purified me and sacrificed me and made me really ready to go to Heaven. I think that this is something, that we must live life beautifully, we have Jesus with us and He loves us. If we could only remember that God loves me, and I have an opportunity to love others as he loves me, not in big things, but in small things with great love, then Norway becomes a nest of love. And how beautiful it will be that from here a centre for peace has been given. That from here the joy of life of the unborn child comes out. If you become a burning light in the world of peace, then really the Nobel Peace Prize is a gift of the Norwegian people. God bless you!

## R.K. NARAYAN

### Abolish Schoolbags

*Delhi, 1986*

*R.K. Narayan (1906–2001) was a leading writer in the English language in India. Many of his stories were set in the fictional south Indian town of Malgudi. He received many awards and honours, and in 1986, he was nominated to the Rajya Sabha, the upper house of the Parliament, where his focus of interest was the plight of schoolchildren across the country. In his maiden speech in the Rajya Sabha, he spoke about the heavy bags children carry to school. It resulted in the formation of a committee to suggest changes to the education system.*

Madam Chairman, I am taking this honourable House to another world. In the stress of concerns of the adult world, the problems or rather the plight of children are unnoticed. I am not referring to any particular class but to childhood itself. The hardship starts right at home when straight from bed the child is pulled out and got ready for school even before his faculties are awake. He or she is groomed and stuffed into a uniform and packed off with a loaded bag on her back. Schoolbag has become an inevitable burden for the child. I am now pleading for abolition of the school bag by an Ordinance, if necessary.

I have investigated and found that an average child carries strapped to his back like a pack-mule, not less than 3–6 kg of books, notebooks and other paraphernalia of modern education in addition to lunch box and water bottles. More children on account of this daily burden develop a stoop and hang their arms forward like a chimpanzee while walking and I know some cases of serious spinal injuries in the children too. Asked why not leave some books behind at home the child replies it is her teacher's order that all books and notes must be brought every day to the class. For what reason,

God alone knows. If there is a lapse, the child invites punishment which takes the form of being rapped on the knuckles with a wooden scale, a refinement from our own days when we received cane cuts on the palm only. The child is in such terror of the teacher whether you call her Sister, 'Mother Superior' or just 'Madam' that she is prepared to carry out any command issued by her who has no imagination or sympathy or whatever.

The dress regulation particularly in convent schools is another senseless formality. Tie, laced shoes and socks, irrespective of the climate is compulsory. Polishing a shoe and lacing it becomes a major task for the child first in the day. When the tie has become an anachronism even in the adult world, it is absurd to enforce it on children. After the school hours, the child returns home only to find her mother or her tutor waiting to pounce upon her, to snatch her bag and compel her to go through special coaching homework. For the child the day has ended with no time for play or to dream. It is a cruel harsh life imposed on her and I present her case before this House and the Honourable Members to think over and devise a remedy by changing the whole educational system and outlook so that childhood has a chance to bloom rather than wilt in the dreadful process of learning.

Other areas where the child needs protection is their involvement in adult activities such as protest marches, parades, lining up on road-side and waiting for VIPs. Children are made to stand in the hot sun for hours without anyone noticing how they suffer from fatigue, hunger and thirst. Children must be protected and cherished which would seem especially relevant in the year of Nehru Centenary. Now, how it is to be done, it is up to the rulers and administrators to consider but perhaps not by appointing a commission of inquiry but in some other practical and peaceful manner.

## MEDHA PATKAR AND BABA AMTE

### We Will Drown, We Will Not Move

*1991*

*Medha Patkar and Baba Amte were awarded the Right Livelihood Award in 1991 for their work on the Narmada Bachao Andolan. Baba Amte (1914–2008) was one of India's most respected social workers who worked for the rehabilitation and empowerment of people suffering from leprosy. Medha Patkar (b. 1954) is one of the initiators of the Narmada Bachao Andolan that has been mobilizing against the Narmada Dam project and aiming to shift the focus to empowerment of the poor and sustainable models of development. This speech was given by Medha Patkar while receiving the award in December 1991.*

More than one hundred and fifty thousand people in and around the bountiful and peaceful valley of Narmada are forced to raise a struggle of life and death. After a long period and an unforgettable process devoted to knowing the dam and the dam-builders, they have declared a total opposition to their uprootment and to its root cause, the Sardar Sarovar project. And to every other such unjust and destructive mega-project, along with the anti-people, non-sustainable policies of natural resource development and distribution that it symbolizes!

They are tribal and poor people, farmers and labourers, fishermen and forest-produce gatherers, small enterprisers and artisans, belonging to about 250 communities. They are socially and economically disadvantaged. The tribal—adivasis, the aborigines—mostly living far from the market and centres of economic and political power; and yet self-reliant, least monetized, and integrated with the forest, a rich natural resource-base, their life-support. Those in the plains have prime agricultural land support. They are united through the generations by the rich habitat, the Narmada Valley; and now by sharing an unprecedented catastrophe. Today they have risen as one man to fight the gigantic forces representing the short-sighted, power-hungry politicians, the self-centered supine bureaucracy, the rapacious contractors, neo-colonial lending agencies and the vulgar consumerist elite population.

The fight has not been an easy one. The tribal people have had to walk down hundreds of kilometres crossing rugged mountain ranges, and men and also women have come out on the streets for protest actions and mass-politics hitherto unknown to them. While initially they had had to run from village to the World Bank compelled to discover the devastative onslaught on their life and livelihood being planned without their knowledge; later they were taken as a threat to the illegitimate and inhuman plans and policies that favour a handful of vested interest.

Since then, the peaceful agitators from the valley have had to face hell: the brutal caning and other forms of force, false legal accusations and arrests, cheating and other ill treatment in the extravagant campaign against the movement, disrespect and deception, insensitivity and unexpected callousness even toward their right to life and their fight for the same.

And the situation has not improved, but rather worsened during the last few months. Today 300 or more people—men and women, young and old from the villages—are in jail for no [fault] of theirs, but for having taken to the most non-violent way of protest within the boundaries of their own village against the dam-related survey work undertaken with the help of 100 policemen armed with slings, tear gas shells and guns. Of course they would not mind courting fearless arrests with conviction and dignity, but they were certainly not prepared to take the vulgar oral abuse of women agitators, unjustifiable beating of men and women even 70-80 years old, and such things which happened between 21st and 30th of November, 1991. But the most disgusting and condemnable action would be what the governments of Gujarat and Maharashtra have planned for the next few days: forcible eviction with police and bulldozing of the families of Manibeli, and of the idol in the oldest Shiva temple of Shurpaneshwar, located in Manibeli.

The most critical phase is ahead of us, and the commitment of our save or drown squads to the resolve *doobenge per nahin hatenge*—'Will drown but not move'—will be put to test during the next few months.

But they are not alone. Similar struggles are on in the other valleys and hills. Tehri and Suvarnarekha in India; Kedung Ombo in Indonesia; Bulbino in Brazil. People in the rural and tribal regions are compelled to justify their survival; establish their right to the traditional, generations-old source of livelihood; protect their properties, community life and culture from the encroachers—not just the colonialist consumerist societies outside and within their nation state, but also the State itself as the wildest and the biggest encroacher.

It is at this moment that the struggle is being recognized as a symbolic guiding force in the terms of the perspective propounded and the people's power expressed. We accept the Right Livelihood Award with all the humility at our command as an expression of solidarity and support to the cause. The perspective which the Award propagates is clear from its motto. The most respected words of the leader of our beloved country, India, Mahatma Gandhi: 'The world has enough for everyone's need but not for anyone's greed'.

We accept this prestigious honour with a feeling of unprecedented responsibility to fight not just against the SSP and other large dams in the Narmada Valley, but also to propound just and sustainable development through a worldwide movement.

The Narmada Bachao Andolan, today, would earnestly request the world community to acknowledge the fact that Sardar Sarovar (SSP) and such projects are unjust and unjustifiable human and environmental devastation. They are conceived and pushed ahead not as the optimum and inevitable solution to the problems of water and energy, but through decisions guided by political expediency. They involve large-scale displacement of not just thousands of families, but of communities; even a tiny 'civilization'. They are claimed to have been appraised but that is within a faulty framework of costs and benefits (like a GNP without a measure of environmental degradation), and exercise of manipulated data-generation and distorted valuations. They swallow large chunks of our millennia-old capital: land, forest, water, cultural and archaeological sites and monuments; and drain financial resources, giving some greening and glowing benefits but for a much shorter period than expected. They cannot be built unless the people in the valleys are cheated by enforcing unjust modern laws and unless their valiant struggles for right to life are crushed!

It is not the SSP and such centralized projects of water supply and hydro power generation—but a decentralized, people-oriented participatory strategy of land and water management, and varied sustainable ways of energy generation (with biomass and human population too) with conservation strategy—that would assure life and livelihood to the millions of people in this world and generations to come.

Sardar Sarovar, the focus of opposition, is the largest out of thirty major irrigation and hydro power projects, with 3,165 other dams proposed to be built in the Valley of Narmada. The decision on this dam, it is said, was made through various investigating committees and the tribunal. The tribunal especially considered the views of the three states—Gujarat, Madhya Pradesh and Maharashtra—represented by their chief ministers and bureaucrats aiming at resolution of the political conflict. But in no way were the tribal and peasant communities and their riparian rights to—or even their unique and non-replaceable relation with—their mother Narmada, taken into consideration. The mute nature and powerless inhabitants of the Valley never were among the parties.

And so the Project goes on...even when the sanctions under the law of our land are withdrawn by the official authority, when Independent Review initiated by the World Bank is on, when the people in the valley are not ready to move out even if to die... With only 10 per cent of the enormous Rs 1,20,000 million or more spent, no doubt the death trap is being set but the neck is still out. It is still not too late. The world of commons—if not the houses and parliaments, the ministers and conferences—have no choice but to take a pause, listen and act.

Today it's the voice of the struggle, singing; tomorrow it will be the death bell ringing.

The world today is facing a challenge that is becoming increasingly acute day by day. For years and decades a few dominant countries and a small elite population in each developing country have ruled the world, exploited the human and material resources, in their favour. When the oppressed and the deprived have begun raising their voice on issues beyond immediate relief and gain.

The problems and the struggles, no doubt, are discussed in various reports and will find place in the UN conference in 1992. But despite this superfluous superstructure the reality on the ground makes us not just worried but impatient.

What has a country like India done to itself, following Western economy and policy blindly? We have come to destroy 50 per cent or more of our land allowing it to degrade because of the cash crop pesticide-fertilizer economy that is geared to international markets.

Our forest wealth has been reduced to less than 10 per cent of our landmass. All this has an unavoidable economic impact that make the poorest and the downtrodden face the backlash of the very development that is justified in the name of equity and justice.

But our rising GNP cares not to reflect this harm and loss. The magnitude of our unirrigated land and unused water bodies are 'used' by our government and the interested lenders. But only we, the people of India, know how and why many of our avowed irrigation and water-supply schemes either become non-functional or have benefits directed to the 'no priority' luxury industries. Our list of 'No water source villages' on the contrary has kept growing. For a few more decades we may be able to boast of self-reliance in cereals. But we certainly feel ashamed to announce the starvation deaths.

We look forward to the twenty-first century and the world economy but unfortunately not the hungry thirsty millions dragging behind. We have a growing chain of five-star hotels with queues in their backyards of ill-fed children, the pillars of our future. This is in almost every country in the third sector, including South America. Blindly awaiting a stroke of fortune called development and modernization. All that comes on the way is to be borne as the inevitable, and left more and more donors to the World Bank and the IMF to tackle.

All this needs to be checked if we care for realization of the values of equity and justice. [If] the vast majority of our population is to be fed and clothed then a balanced vision with our own priorities in place of the Western models is a must. The latter indicate dehumanization of populations through machines, an increasing rift between man and nature and a civilization in a hurry to exploit their and others natural capital without a place to dump their waste. Their disrespect for indigenous communities is to be remembered on the eve of the 500th anniversary of Columbus not discovering, but conquering, America. Their colonial and neo-colonial ambitions continue to exploit the nation states through manoeuvred politics of international aid. The multilateral-agencies-aided mega projects are adjusted sectors—even education have been the tools.

There is no other way but to redefine 'modernity' and the goals of development, not to narrow it to 'environment' but to widen it to a sustainable, equitable, just society based on harmonious non-exploitative relationship between human being to human being, and human being to nature. We cannot be either politically naive or apathetic or playing the unseen hand of free economy.

The victims of development are to be reached out to, mobilized and organized into non-party movements of political relevance, based on people's empowerment and people's politics with a new political ideology and consciousness, [we] may call it Environmental Democratic Socialism.

Not just green, but green and red ideas together can lead us to the right livelihood. The seeds of this are still alive in many tribal societies which cannot be allowed to [become] extinct. They have to say 'NO' to plundering their natural capital and cultural wealth if the world is to behave. Bows and arrows will not help. Non-violent opposition to the uncivilized traditions of big dams and mega projects like Narmada, with our souls converted into weapons, ready to defend our way of life, till our bodies are flushed out, can be our humble attempt not just to save the eternal Valley but the questions of humankind.

## ATAL BIHARI VAJPAYEE

### The Power of the Printed Word

*New Delhi, 2000*

*Atal Bihari Vajpayee (1924–2018) is a former prime minister of India. He was first elected to the Lok Sabha in 1957, and spent close to four decades as a Member of Parliament. Throughout his career, he was known for his erudite speeches and also his poetry. Following is the speech he delivered on 5 February 2000 at the inauguration of the fourteenth World Book Fair in Delhi. In this speech, he spoke about the various ways in which books enrich our lives.*

I am happy to be here this morning to inaugurate the fourteenth World Book Fair organized by the National Book Trust of India. Over the years, this biennial event has become popular among both book-lovers and publishers. The World Book Fair is now a gathering point for publishers from India and abroad.

A book fair, however, is more than a trade event or a meeting place for booksellers and publishers. A book fair, more so a world book fair, provides an opportunity to the people to keep track of new ideas and perspectives.

For, books are like windows that open up to the limitless world of knowledge. They encourage us to think and expand our horizon. They are the source of education and intellectual inspiration. Indeed, books serve to enlighten society and, throughout human history, have proved to be more powerful than weapons of death and destruction.

It is, therefore, not surprising that history is replete with instances of burning of books and sacking of libraries to subjugate people and establish political, racial or religious supremacy. The power of knowledge, of ideas, of imagination, has always scared those whose strength derives from bigotry and fundamentalism.

We have seen books being burned from Berlin to Bradford. We have seen books being banned and authors persecuted. But neither burning nor banning has been able to suppress the human mind—ideas have survived, new ideas are being born and the quest for knowledge continues.

Books, as we know them today, date back to the advent of the printing press. Before that they existed as hand-written texts. And, even before that, there was the oral tradition. In the beginning, of course, there was shabda, the word, as Brahma, the inner soul. Reverence for knowledge and dharma came to be identified with reverence for the book.

India can boast of a rich oral tradition, dating back many millennia to the composition of the Vedas and Upanishads. Sruti was the means of handing down through generations our ancient texts over centuries. Sruti was that which was heard and realized. It was literature that sought to both enlighten the individual as well as serve the interests of the community.

For instance, the Vedas are as much an instrument of salvation of the individual soul as the prosperity and well-being of the community at large. That oral tradition was to later transform itself into the written tradition. First came the palm-leaf manuscript. Later paper was used. Much later came the printing press.

The spoken word of the oral tradition was restricted to those to whom it was passed on. The pothis [old manuscripts], for obvious reasons, had limited access. The printing press, however, had a revolutionary impact—millions of people today have access to what was in the beginning shabda.

From serving the basic needs of communicating fundamentals to a child, and thus teaching the child to read and write, a book today serves many purposes. But the common factor of all these purposes still remains the same as that of the oral tradition: disseminating knowledge, basic and specialized. Knowledge that flows from ideas; knowledge that stems from experience; and, knowledge that is born of discoveries. Above all, knowledge that lifts the darkness of ignorance, intolerance and inwardness.

The revolution that was brought about by the printing press has yielded place to yet another revolution. The advent of new technology has provided us with new vehicles of knowledge dissemination. Ideas, images and impressions, instead of leaping out from the pages of a book, now leap out at you from computer screens. Today, instead of reading a book, you can hear an audio book. In fact, while audio books, at one level, take us back to our oral tradition, at another level, they have made it possible for those who, for a variety of reasons, can neither read nor write, to access knowledge. We are also witnessing a fast shift towards electronic journals which can be accessed by millions of people courtesy the information superhighway. A book, therefore, no longer need exist in physical form or between covers.

Will books, then, become extinct? Will libraries disappear and leave us with formless digital volumes that will exist in the netherworld of cyber space? Will the turning of pages be replaced by the clicking of mouses?

Similar apprehensions were experienced with the advent of television, when newspapers wondered whether they would soon cease to exist. But we have seen the power of the printed word which has survived the onslaught of the audio-visual image. I have no doubt that printed books will survive the cyber age.

To ensure that survival, however, publishers have to play an important role. Books have to be made affordable so that individual buyers are not constrained by the price line. I do understand that the cost of printing a book has increased over the years. I am happy that this is partly due to the fact that authors have begun to receive their fair share.

One way of overcoming the problem of high prices is to strengthen the system of public libraries. I would urge people not to look forward to official patronage for setting up huge libraries that invariably become unwieldy and inaccessible to the masses. Residential colonies and communities should set up their own libraries. Not only will these be more accessible to the common people, especially children, but they will also foster a sense of community participation in making books available to all. This experiment has been tried successfully in West Bengal, where numerous community-run libraries exist, catering to all age groups. I also call upon schools to spend more on their libraries so that the habit of reading can be inculcated among children in their formative years.

I would also like to urge Indian publishers to invest more in publishing books written in all Indian languages. There are fine authors who write in Indian languages and greater effort is called for to make their work available to readers from other regions. Simultaneously, efforts should be made to translate their work into English so that a larger number of people, both in India and abroad, have access to their books. Once again this is an area where publishers can, and should, play a significant role.

I thank the organizers of the fourteenth World Book Fair for this opportunity to share some of my thoughts with you. I wish publishers, authors and booksellers a successful gathering at this fair.

Thank you.

## A.P.J. ABDUL KALAM

### The Teachers Who Shaped My Life

*New Delhi, 2003*

*A.P.J. Abdul Kalam (1931–2015) was a scientist and the eleventh President of India. As a scientist, he worked on India's satellite systems as well as missile systems. He served as the President of India from 2001 to 2007, earning great love from the people, especially students and young people everywhere. He was called the 'People's President' by many. He spoke and wrote extensively on education, equality and the determination to succeed. These are excerpts from his address over All India Radio on the eve of Teacher's Day, September 2003.*

Dear listeners of All India Radio and teachers, my greetings to all of you.

I am talking to you on the special occasion of Teachers' Day. On this day, we gratefully remember the great educationist Dr Sarvepalli Radhakrishnan, whose dream was that, 'Teachers should be the best minds in the country'. Hence, Teachers' Day is very important for all our people, as the teachers lay the foundation for creating enlightened citizens for the nation. On this day, I would like to recall three teachers who helped me in shaping my life.

To begin with I am going to talk to you about my father Janab Avul Pakir Jainulabdeen, as a teacher. My father taught me a great lesson when I was a young boy. It was just after India got Independence. My father was elected Panchayat Board member and on the same day he was also elected the president of the Rameswaram Panchayat Board. At that time they elected my father as Panchayat Board president not because he belonged to a particular religion or a particular caste or spoke a particular language or for his economic status. He was elected only on the basis of his nobility of mind and for being a good human being. Dear listeners, I would like to narrate one incident that took place on the day he was elected president of the Panchayat Board.

Those days we did not have electricity and we used to study under ration kerosene lamps. I was reading the lessons loudly and I heard a knock at the door. Somebody opened the door, came in and asked me where my father was? I told him that father had gone for the evening namaz. Then he said, I have brought something for him, can I keep it here? I asked the person to leave the item on the cot. After that I continued my studies.

I used to learn by reading aloud in my younger days. I was reading loud and fully concentrating on my studies. At that time my father came in and saw a tambalum kept in the cot. He opened the cover of the tambalum and found there was a costly dhoti, angawastram, some fruits and some sweets and he could see the slip that the person had left behind.

That was the first time I saw him very angry and also that was the first time I had got a thorough beating from him. I got frightened and started weeping. My mother embraced and consoled me. Then my father came and touched my shoulder lovingly with affection and advised me not to receive any gift without his permission. Then he told me that it is not a good habit. A gift is always accompanied by some purpose and a gift is a dangerous thing. It is like touching a snake and getting the poison in turn. This lesson stands out always in my mind even when I am in my seventies.

When I think of my second teacher, I am reminded of my childhood days when I was studying in 8th class at the age of 13. I had a teacher, Shri Siva Subramania Iyer. All of us loved to attend his class. One day he was teaching about a bird's flight. He drew a diagram of a bird on the blackboard depicting the wings, tail and the body structure with the head. He explained how birds create the lift and fly. He also explained to us how they change direction while flying. At the end of the class, he wanted to know whether we understood how birds fly. I said, I did not understand. When I said this, the teacher asked the other students whether they understood or not. Many students said that they also did not understand. He did not get upset by our response since he was a committed teacher.

Our teacher said that he would take all of us to the sea shore. That evening the whole class was at the sea shore of Rameswaram. He showed the sea birds in formations of 10 to 20 numbers. We saw the marvellous formations of birds with a purpose and we were all amazed. He showed us the birds and asked us to see that when the birds fly, what they looked like. We saw the wings flapping. He asked us to look at the tail portion with the combination of flapping wings and twisting tail. We noticed closely and found that the birds in that condition flew in the direction they desired. Then he asked us a question, 'Where is the engine and how is it powered?'

The bird is powered by its own life and the motivation of what it wants. All these things were explained to us within fifteen minutes. We all understood the dynamics from this practical example. Our teacher was a great teacher; he could give us a theoretical lesson coupled with a live practical example available in nature. This is real teaching. I am sure many of the teachers in schools and colleges will follow this example.

From that evening, I thought that my future study has to be with reference to flight and flight systems. I am saying this because my teacher's teaching and the event that I witnessed decided my future career. The bird flying exercise given by my teacher, really gave me a goal and a mission for my life. Thus my life was transformed as a rocket engineer, aerospace engineer and technologist. That one incident of my teacher teaching the lesson, showing the visual live example proved to be a turning point in my life which eventually shaped my profession.

A student during his school life up to 10+2 spends 25,000 hours in the school campus. His life is more influenced by the teachers and the school environment. Therefore, the school must have the best of teachers with ability to teach and love teaching. Teachers should become role models. Similarly, the student must be alert to build himself with best of qualities and to get ignited with a vision for his future life.

I would like to share with you another experience with my teacher Prof. Satish Dhawan. First, I worked in Delhi with the Ministry of Defence. Later I joined the Defence Research and Development Organisation (DRDO) in 1958 at the Aeronautical Development Establishment at Bangalore. There, with the advice of the Director, I took up the development of hovercraft. Hovercraft design needed the development of a ducted contra-rotating propeller for creating a smooth flow balancing the torques. I did not know how to design a contra-rotating propeller though I knew how to design a conventional propeller. Some of my friends told me that I could approach Prof. Satish Dhawan of the Indian Institute of Science, for help.

I took permission from my Director and went to Prof Dhawan who was sitting in a small room in the Indian Institute of Science with a lot of books in the background and a blackboard on the wall. I explained the problem.. He told me that it was really a challenging task and he would teach me the design if I attended his classes from 2 p.m. to 3 p.m. on all Saturdays for the next six weeks.

He was a visionary teacher. He prepared the schedule for the entire course and wrote it on the black board. He also gave me the reference material and books I should read before I start attending the course. Before commencing each meeting, he would ask critical questions and assess my understanding of the subject. That was for the first time that I realized how a good teacher prepares himself for teaching with meticulous planning and prepares the student for acquisition of knowledge. This process continued for the next six weeks. I got the capability for designing the contra-rotating propeller. That was the time I realized that Prof Dhawan was not only a teacher but also a fantastic development engineer of aeronautical systems.

Later during the critical phases of testing, Prof Dhawan was with me to witness the test and find solutions to the problems. After reaching the smooth test phase, the contra-rotating propeller went through 50 hours of continuous testing. Prof Dhawan witnessed the test himself and congratulated me. However, at that time, I did not realize that Prof Dhawan would become chairman, ISRO and that I would get the opportunity to work with him as a project director in the development of the satellite launch vehicle SLV-3 for injecting the Rohini satellite into the orbit. Nature has its own way to link the student's dream and real life later.

This was the first design in my career which gave me the confidence to design many complex aerospace systems in future. Through this project I learnt the techniques of designing and developing the contra-rotating propeller. Above all, I learnt that in a project, problems will always crop up; we should not allow problems to be our masters but we should defeat the problems.

The three teachers in my life; what did they

give me? Any enlightened human being can be created by three unique characteristics. One is moral value system. That I got from my father the hard way. Secondly, the teacher becoming a role model. Not only does the student learn, but the teacher shapes his life with great dreams and aims. Finally, the education and learning process has to culminate in the creation of professional capability leading to confidence and will power to make a design, to make a product, to make a system, bravely combating many problems. What a fortune and blessing I had from my three teachers.

Among the listeners, there may be many parents, many teachers and a large number of students. Every one of us in this planet creates a page in human history irrespective of who he/ she is. I realize my experience is a small dot in human life, but that dot has a life and light. This light, let it light many lamps.

My best wishes to all of you on this occasion of Teachers' Day. Thank you.

## AMARTYA SEN

### The Importance of Basic Education

*Edinburgh, 2003*

*Amartya Sen (b. 1933) is an economist and philosopher. He is the Thomas W. Lamont University Professor at Harvard University and member of faculty at Harvard Law School. He is a Fellow of Trinity College, Cambridge. He was awarded the Nobel Prize in Economic Sciences in 1998 and the Bharat Ratna in 1999. He is the author of a number of books on economics and on India and Indian thought. The speech here is a slightly shortened version of a lecture he gave at the Commonwealth Education Conference in Edinburgh on 18 October 2003. Here he talks about the need for universal basic education and how access to education can bring about extensive and deep changes in society.*

It is a great privilege for me to have the opportunity of speaking at this meeting of Commonwealth countries on education. I am also very happy that you have chosen Edinburgh as the venue of this important conference. I am very proud of my own association with Edinburgh, through being an alumnus of two universities here, Edinburgh University and Heriot-Watt University (admittedly my connections are only through honorary degrees but they generate a sense of closeness to the real students here), and also through belonging to the Royal Society of Edinburgh and having other associations with this great city. So I welcome you to beautiful Edinburgh and to its wonderful intellectual community, of which I am privileged to be a nomadic member, as something of an academic gypsy. But to this welcome I must add my belief that there could not be a better place for a meeting on 'closing the gap' in education than the city of Adam Smith and David Hume, the earliest and greatest champions of education for all.

Why is it so important to close the educational gaps, and to remove the enormous disparities in educational access, inclusion and achievement? One reason, among others, is the importance of this for making the world more secure as well as more fair. H.G. Wells was not exaggerating when he said, in his *Outline of History*: 'Human history becomes more and more a race between education and catastrophe.' If we continue to leave vast sections of the people of the world outside the orbit of education, we make the world not only less just, but also less secure.

The precariousness of the world is now greater than it already was in H.G. Wells's time in early twentieth century. Indeed, since the terrible events of 11 September 2001—and what followed after that—the world has been very aware of problems of physical insecurity. But human insecurity comes in many different ways—not just through terrorism and violence. Indeed, even on the very day of 11 September 2001, more people died from AIDS than from physical violence, including the atrocity in New York. Human insecurity can develop in many different ways, and physical violence is only one of them. While it is important to fight terrorism and genocide (and in this too, education can have a big role, as I will presently discuss), we must also recognize the plural nature of human insecurity and its diverse manifestations.

As it happens, widening the coverage and effectiveness of basic education can have a powerfully preventive role in reducing human insecurity of nearly every kind. It is useful to consider briefly the different ways in which removing discrepancies and neglects in education can contribute to reducing human insecurity across the world.

The most basic issue relates to the elementary fact that illiteracy and innumeracy are forms of insecurity in themselves. Not to be able to read or write or count or communicate is a tremendous deprivation. The extreme case of insecurity is the certainty of deprivation, and the absence of any chance of avoiding that fate. The first and most immediate contribution of successful school education is a direct reduction of this basic deprivation—this extreme insecurity—which continues to ruin the lives of a large part of the global population, not least in the Commonwealth.

The difference that basic education can make to human life is easy to see. It is also readily appreciated even by the poorest of families. Speaking personally, it has been wonderful for me to observe how easily the importance of education is perceived even by the poorest and the most deprived of families. This emerges from some studies on primary education in India that we are currently undertaking (through the 'Pratichi Trust'—a trust aimed at basic education and gender equity that I have been privileged to set up in India and Bangladesh through using my Nobel Prize money from 1998). As the results of our studies come in, it is remarkable to find how the parents from even the poorest and most depressed families long to give basic education to their children, to make them grow up without the terrible handicaps from which they—the parents—had themselves suffered.

Indeed, contrary to claims often made, we have not observed any basic reluctance by parents to send their children—daughters as well as boys—to school, provided affordable, effective and safe schooling opportunities actually exist in their neighbourhood. Of course, there are many obstacles in giving shape to the dreams of parents. The economic circumstances of the families often make it very hard for them to send their children to school, particularly when there are fees to be paid.

The obstacle of unaffordability must be firmly removed across the Commonwealth—indeed the world. I am, of course, aware that some champions of the market system want to leave school fees to the market forces. But this cannot but be a mistake given the social obligation to give the essential opportunity of schooling to all children. Indeed, Adam Smith, who provided the classic analysis of the power and reach of the market mechanism two and quarter centuries ago, wrote eloquently, sitting in Kirkcaldy (not far from here), why it would be wrong to leave this to the market:

'For a very small expence the publick can facilitate, can encourage, and can even impose upon almost the whole body of the people, the necessity of acquiring those most essential parts of education.'

There are other obstacles too. Sometimes the schools are very thinly staffed (many primary schools in developing countries have only one teacher), and parents are often worried about the safety of children, especially girl children (particularly in case the teacher fails to turn up, which seems to happen often enough in many of the poorer countries). Quite often, the parents' reluctance has a rational basis, and these gaps too need to be addressed.

There are other barriers as well. Very poor families often rely on labour contributions from everyone, even the children, and this can compete with the demands of schooling. This unfortunate practice, though generated out of hardship, must also be removed, through regulation as well as by making the economic benefits of schooling clearer to all. This brings us to the second issue in understanding the contribution of schooling in removing human insecurity. Basic education can be very important in helping people to get jobs and gainful employment. This economic connection, while always present, is particularly critical in a rapidly globalizing world in which quality control and production according to strict specification can be crucial.

Not surprisingly, all the cases of speedy use of the opportunities of global commerce for the reduction of poverty have drawn on help from basic education on a wide basis. For example, in Japan, already in the mid-nineteenth century the task was seen with remarkable clarity. The Fundamental Code of Education, issued in 1872 (shortly after the Meiji restoration in 1868), expressed the public commitment to make sure that there must be 'no community with an illiterate family, nor a family with an illiterate person'. Thus—with the closing of educational gaps—began Japan's remarkable history of rapid economic development. By 1910 Japan was almost fully literate, at least for the young, and by 1913, though still very much poorer than Britain or America, Japan was publishing more books than Britain and more than twice as many as the United States. The concentration on education determined, to a large extent, the nature and speed of Japan's economic and social progress.

Later on, particularly in the second half of the twentieth century, South Korea, China, Taiwan, Hong Kong, Singapore, and other economies in East Asia followed similar routes and firmly focused on general expansion of education. Widespread participation in a global economy would have been hard to accomplish if people could not read or write, or produce according to specifications or instructions, or to have quality control.

Third, when people are illiterate, their ability to understand and invoke their legal rights can be very limited, and educational neglect can also lead to other kinds of deprivation. Indeed, this tends to be a persistent problem for people at the bottom of the ladder, whose rights are often effectively alienated because of their inability to read and see what they are entitled to demand and how. The educational gap clearly has a class connection.

It also has a gender connection since it can be a very important issue for women's security. Women are often deprived of their due, thanks to illiteracy. Not being able to read or write is a significant barrier for underprivileged women, since this can lead to their failure to make use even of the rather limited rights they may legally have (say, to own land, or other property, or to appeal against unfair judgment and unjust treatment). There are often legal rights in rulebooks that are not used because the aggrieved parties cannot read those rulebooks. Gaps in schooling can, thus, directly lead to insecurity by distancing the deprived from the ways and means of fighting against that deprivation.

Fourth, illiteracy can also muffle the political opportunities of the underdog, by reducing their ability to participate in political arena and to express their demands effectively. This can contribute directly to their insecurity, since the absence of voice in politics can entail a severe reduction of influence and the likelihood of just treatment of those who are kept on the wrong side of the gap.

Fifth, basic education can play a major role in tackling health problems in general and epidemics in particular. It is easy to see the importance of specialized health education (for example, on the way infections spread and how diseases can be prevented). But even general education can broaden a person's lines of thinking and generate social understanding in ways that may be extremely important in facing epidemiological problems. Indeed, some studies have suggested that general school education has a bigger impact on health than specialized health education itself has.

Sixth, empirical work in recent years has

brought out very clearly how the relative respect and regard for women's well-being is strongly influenced by women's literacy and educated participation in decisions within and outside the family. Even the survival disadvantage of women compared with men in many developing countries (which leads to such terrible phenomenon as a hundred million of 'missing women') seems to go down sharply—and may even get eliminated—with progress in women's empowerment, for which literacy is a basic ingredient.

There is also considerable evidence that fertility rates tend to go down sharply with greater empowerment of women. This is not surprising, since the lives that are most battered by the frequent bearing and rearing of children are those of young women, and anything that enhances their decisional power and increases the attention that their interests receive tends, in general, to prevent over-frequent child bearing. For example, in a comparative study of the different districts within India, it has clearly emerged that women's education and women's employment are the two most important influences in reducing fertility rates. In that extensive study, female education and employment are the only variables that have a statistically significant impact in explaining variations in fertility rates across more than three hundred districts that make up India. In understanding inter-regional differences, for example the fact the state of Kerala in India has a fertility rate of only 1.7 (which can be roughly interpreted as 1.7 children on average per couple) in contrast with many areas which have four children per couple (or even more), the level of female education provides the most effective explanation.

There is also much evidence that women's education and literacy tend to reduce the mortality rates of children. These and other connections between basic education of women and the power of women's agency (and its extensive reach) indicate why the gender gap in education produces heavy social penalties.

I have so far concentrated on gaps in access, inclusion and achievement that differentiate one group of people from another. But this is also a good occasion to reflect a little on the gaps—of a very different kind—that exist in the coverage of the school curriculum. The nature of the curriculum is, of course, of obvious relevance to the development of technical skills (such as computing) that facilitate participation in the contemporary world. But there are also other issues involved, since schooling can be deeply influential in the identity of a person and the way we see ourselves and each other.

This issue has received some attention recently in the special context of the role of fundamentalist religious schools, and there is need to pay attention to the narrowing of horizons, especially of children, that illiberal and intolerant education can produce. It is also important to recognize that lack of public facilities for the schooling of children often contributes greatly to the appeal and popularity of religious schools run by political militants.

Indeed, the nature of education is quite central to peace in the world. Recently the very deceptive perspective of the so-called 'clash of civilizations' (championed particularly by Samuel Huntington) has gained much currency. It is important to see that what is most immediately divisive in this kind of theorizing is not the silly idea of the inevitability of a clash (that too, but it comes later), but the equally shallow prior insistence on seeing human beings in terms of one dimension only, regarding them just as members of one civilization or another (defined mostly in terms of religion), ignoring their other affiliations and involvements.

There are two mistakes here. First, the classification is very crude. For example, India is put in the box of Hindu civilization, even though with its 130 million Muslims (more than the entire British and French populations put together), India has many more Muslims than most so-called 'Muslim countries' in the world. Huntington's classification gives comfort only to Hindu sectarians.

The second mistake is to assume that a person's religion defines him or her reasonably adequately. But every human being's identities have many different components, related to nationality, language, location, class, occupation, history, religion, political beliefs, and so on. A Bangladeshi Muslim is not only a Muslim, but also a Bengali and possibly quite proud of the richness of the Bengali literature and other cultural achievements. Similarly, the history of the Arab world with which an Arab child today can potentially relate is not only the achievements of Islam (important as they are), but also the great secular accomplishments in mathematics, science and literature which are part and parcel of Arab history. Even today when a scientist in, say, the Imperial College uses an 'algorithm', he or she unconsciously celebrates the innovativeness of the ninth-century Arab mathematician, Al-Khwarizmi, from whose name the term algorithm is derived (the term 'algebra' comes from his book, *Al Jabr wa-al-Muqabilah*).

To define people just in terms of religion-based classification of civilizations can itself contribute to political insecurity, since in this view people are seen as simply belonging to, say, 'the Muslim world', or 'the Western world', or 'the Hindu world', or 'the Buddhist world', and so on. To ignore everything other than religion in classifying people is to set people up in potentially belligerent camps. I personally believe that even the UK government makes a mistake in expanding, rather than reducing faith-based state schools, adding for example Muslim schools, Hindu schools and Sikh schools to pre-existing Christian ones, especially when the new religious schools leave children very little opportunity to cultivate reasoned choice and decide how the various components of their identities (related respectively to language, literature, religion, ethnicity, cultural history, scientific interests, etc) should receive attention. There is need not only to discuss the importance of our common humanity, but also to stress the fact that our diversities can take many distinct forms and that we have to use our reasoning to decide how to see ourselves.

The importance of non-sectarian and non-parochial curricula that expand, rather than reduce, the reach of reason can be hard to exaggerate. Shakespeare talked about the fact that 'some men are born great, some achieve greatness, and some have greatness thrust upon them'. In the schooling of children, we have to make sure that we do not have smallness thrust upon the young.

## SUBROTO BAGCHI

### Go, Kiss the World

*Bangalore, 2006*

*Subroto Bagchi (b. 1957) is an entrepreneur and business leader. He is co-founder of the IT company Mindtree. He is also the best-selling author of a number of business books. He gave this speech to the graduating class of Indian Institute of Management, Bangalore, in 2006. In this inspiring speech he talks of his growing up years, the struggle of his parents, their unflinching honesty and the lessons he learnt from them that helped him even as an entrepreneur and business person.*

I was the last child of a small-time government servant, in a family of five brothers. My earliest memory of my father is as that of a District Employment Officer in Koraput, Orissa. It was, and remains as back of beyond as you can imagine. There was no electricity; no primary school nearby and water did not flow out of a tap. As a result, I did not go to school until the age of eight; I was home-schooled. My father used to get transferred every year. The family belongings fit into the back of a jeep—so the family moved from place to place and without any trouble, my mother would set up an establishment and get us going. Raised by a widow who had come as a refugee from the then East Bengal, she was a matriculate when she married my father.

My parents set the foundation of my life and the value system, which makes me what I am today and largely defines what success means to me today.

As District Employment Officer, my father was given a jeep by the government. There was no garage in the office, so the jeep was parked in our house. My father refused to use it to commute to the office. He told us that the jeep is an expensive resource given by the government—he reiterated to us that it was not 'his jeep' but the government's jeep. Insisting that he would use it only to tour the interiors, he would walk to his office on normal days. He also made sure that we never sat in the government jeep—we could sit in it only when it was stationary.

That was our early childhood lesson in governance—a lesson that corporate managers learn the hard way, some never do.

The driver of the jeep was treated with respect due to any other member of my father's office. As small children, we were taught not to call him by his name. We had to use the suffix 'dada' whenever we were to refer to him in public or private. When I grew up to own a car and a driver by the name of Raju was appointed—I repeated the lesson to my two small daughters. They have, as a result, grown up to call Raju, 'Raju Uncle'—very different from many of their friends who refer to their family driver, as 'my driver'. When I hear that term from a school— or college-going person, I cringe.

To me, the lesson was significant—you treat small people with more respect than how you treat big people. It is more important to respect your subordinates than your superiors.

Our day used to start with the family huddling around my mother's chulha—an earthen fire place she would build at each place of posting where she would cook for the family. There was neither gas, nor electrical stoves. The morning routine started with tea. As the brew was served, father would ask us to read aloud the editorial page of *The Statesman*'s 'muffosil' edition—delivered one day late. We did not understand much of what we were reading. But the ritual was meant for us to know that the world was larger than Koraput district and the English I speak today, despite having studied in an Oriya medium school, has to do with that routine. After reading the newspaper aloud, we were told to fold it neatly. Father taught us a simple lesson.

He used to say, 'You should leave your newspaper and your toilet the way you expect to find it.' That lesson was about showing consideration to others. Business begins and ends with that simple precept.

Being small children, we were always enamoured with advertisements in the newspaper for transistor radios—we did not have one. We saw other people having radios in their homes and each time there was an advertisement of Philips, Murphy or Bush radios, we would ask Father when we could get one. Each time, my father would reply that we did not need one because he already had five radios—alluding to his five sons.

We also did not have a house of our own and would occasionally ask father as to when, like others, we would live in our own house. He would give a similar reply, 'We do not need a house of our own. I already own five houses.' His replies did not gladden our hearts in that instant.

Nonetheless, we learnt that it is important not to measure personal success and sense of well-being through material possessions.

Government houses seldom came with fences. Mother and I collected twigs and built a small fence. After lunch, my mother would never sleep. She would take her kitchen utensils and with those she and I would dig the rocky, white ant-infested surrounding. We planted flowering bushes. The white ants destroyed them. My mother brought ash from her chulha and mixed it in the earth and we planted the seedlings all over again. This time, they bloomed. At that time, my father's transfer order came. A few neighbours told my mother why she was taking so much pain to beautify a government house, why she was planting seeds that would only benefit the next occupant. My mother replied that it did not matter to her that she would not see the flowers in full bloom. She said, 'I have to create a bloom in a desert and whenever I am given a new place, I must leave it more beautiful than what I had inherited.'

That was my first lesson in success. It is not about what you create for yourself, it is what you leave behind that defines success.

My mother began developing a cataract in her eyes when I was very small. At that time, the eldest among my brothers got a teaching job at the University in Bhubaneswar and had to prepare for the civil services examination. So, it was decided that my mother would move to cook for him and, as her appendage, I had to move too. For the first time in my life I saw electricity in homes and water coming out of a tap. It was around 1965 and the country was going to war with Pakistan. My mother was having problems reading and in any case, being Bengali, she did not know the Oriya script. So, in addition to my daily chores, my job was to read her the local newspaper—end to end. That created in me a sense of connectedness with a larger world. I began taking interest in many different things. While reading out news about the war, I felt that I was fighting the war myself. She and I discussed the daily news and built a bond with the larger universe. In it, we became part of a larger reality. Till date, I measure my success in terms of that sense of larger connectedness. Meanwhile, the war raged and India was fighting on both fronts. Lal Bahadur Shastri, the then Prime Minster, coined the term 'Jai Jawan, Jai Kishan' and galvanized the nation into patriotic fervour. Other than reading out the newspaper to my mother, I had no clue about how I could be part of the action. So, after reading her the newspaper, every day I would land up near the University's water tank, which served the community. I would spend hours under it, imagining that there could be spies who would come to poison the water and I had to watch for them. I would daydream about catching one and how the next day, I would be featured in the newspaper. Unfortunately for me, the spies at war ignored the sleepy town of Bhubaneswar and I never got a chance to catch one in action. Yet, that act unlocked my imagination.

Imagination is everything. If we can imagine a future, we can create it, if we can create that future, others will live in it. That is the essence of success.

Over the next few years, my mother's eyesight dimmed but in me she created a larger vision, a vision with which I continue to see the world and, I sense, through my eyes, she was seeing too. As the next few years unfolded, her vision deteriorated and she was operated for cataract. I remember, when she returned after her operation and she saw my face clearly for the first time, she was astonished. She said, 'Oh my God, I did not know you were so fair.' I remain mighty pleased with that adulation even till date. Within weeks of getting her sight back, she developed a corneal ulcer and, overnight, became blind in both eyes. That was 1969. She died in 2002. In all those 32 years of living with blindness, she never complained about her fate even once. Curious to know what she saw with blind eyes, I asked her once if she sees darkness. She replied, 'No, I do not see darkness. I only see light even with my eyes closed.' Until she was eighty years of age, she did her morning yoga everyday, swept her own room and washed her own clothes.

To me, success is about the sense of independence; it is about not seeing the world but seeing the light.

Over the many intervening years, I grew up, studied, joined the industry and began to carve my life's own journey. I began my life as a clerk in a government office, went on to become a management trainee with the DCM group and eventually found my life's calling with the IT industry when fourth generation computers came to India in 1981. Life took me places—I worked with outstanding people, challenging assignments and travelled all over the world.

In 1992, while I was posted in the US, I learnt that my father, living a retired life with my eldest brother, had suffered a third degree burn injury and was admitted in the Safdarjung Hospital in Delhi. I flew back to attend to him—he remained for a few days in critical stage, bandaged from neck to toe. The Safdarjung Hospital is a cockroach infested, dirty, inhuman place. The overworked, under-resourced sisters in the burn ward are both victims and perpetrators of dehumanized life at its worst. One morning, while attending to my father, I realized that the blood bottle was empty and fearing that air would go into his vein, I asked the attending nurse to change it. She bluntly told me to do it myself. In that horrible theater of death, I was in pain and frustration and anger. Finally when she relented and came, my father opened his eyes and murmured to her, 'Why have you not gone home yet?' Here was a man on his deathbed but more concerned about the overworked nurse than his own state. I was stunned at his stoic self.

There I learnt that there is no limit to how concerned you can be for another human being and what the limit of inclusion is you can create.

My father died the next day. He was a man whose success was defined by his principles, his frugality, his universalism and his sense of inclusion.

Above all, he taught me that success is your ability to rise above your discomfort, whatever may be your current state. You can, if you want, raise your consciousness above your immediate surroundings. Success is not about building material comforts—the transistor that he never could buy or the house that he never owned. His success was about the legacy he left, the memetic continuity of his ideals that grew beyond the smallness of an ill-paid, unrecognized government servant's world.

My father was a fervent believer in the British Raj. He sincerely doubted the capability of the post-independence Indian political parties to govern the country. To him, the lowering of the Union Jack was a sad event. My mother was the exact opposite. When Subhash Bose quit the Indian National Congress and came to Dhaka, my mother, then a schoolgirl, garlanded him. She learnt to spin khadi and joined an underground movement that trained her in using daggers and swords. Consequently, our household saw diversity in the political outlook of the two. On major issues concerning the world, the Old Man and the Old Lady had differing opinions.

In them, we learnt the power of disagreements, of dialogue and the essence of living with diversity in thinking.

Success is not about the ability to create a definitive dogmatic end state; it is about the unfolding of thought processes, of dialogue and continuum.

Two years back, at the age of eighty-two, Mother had a paralytic stroke and was lying in a government hospital in Bhubaneswar. I flew down from the US where I was serving my second stint, to see her. I spent two weeks with her in the hospital as she remained in a paralytic state. She was neither getting better nor moving on. Eventually I had to return to work. While leaving her behind, I kissed her face. In that paralytic state and a garbled voice, she said, 'Why are you kissing me, go kiss the world.' Her river was nearing its journey, at the confluence of life and death, this woman who came to India as a refugee, raised by a widowed mother, no more educated than high school, married to an anonymous government servant whose last salary was rupees three hundred, robbed of her eyesight by fate and crowned by adversity was telling me to go and kiss the world!

Success to me is about *vision*. It is the ability to rise above the immediacy of pain. It is about imagination. It is about sensitivity to small people. It is about building inclusion. It is about connectedness to a larger world existence. It is about personal tenacity. It is about giving back more to life than you take out of it. It is about creating extraordinary success with ordinary lives.

Thank you very much; I wish you good luck and godspeed. Go! Kiss the world.

## RAHUL DRAVID

### What Does Cricket Mean in India

*Canberra, 2011*

*Rahul Dravid (b.1973) is a cricketer and former India team captain. He is widely regarded as one of the greatest batsmen in the world and holds a number of cricketing records. He was nicknamed The Wall for his consistency on the field. In December 2011, he was the first non-Australian to deliver the Bradman Oration in Canberra. Following are excerpts from the speech.*

Thank you for inviting me to deliver the Bradman Oration; the respect and the regard that came with the invitation to speak tonight are deeply appreciated.

I realize a very distinguished list of gentlemen have preceded me in the ten years that the Bradman Oration has been held. I know that this Oration is held every year to appreciate the life and career of Sir Don Bradman, a great Australian and a great cricketer. I understand that I am supposed to speak about cricket and issues in the game—and I will.

Yet, but first before all else, I must say that I find myself humbled by the venue we find ourselves in. Even though there is neither a pitch in sight, nor stumps or bat and balls, as a cricketer, I feel I stand on very sacred ground tonight. When I was told that I would be speaking at the National War Memorial, I thought of how often and how meaninglessly, the words 'war', 'battle', 'fight' are used to describe cricket matches.

Yes, we cricketers devote the better part of our adult lives to being prepared to perform for our countries, to persist and compete as intensely as we can—and more. This building, however, recognizes the men and women who lived out the words—war, battle, fight—for real and then gave it all up for their country, their lives left incomplete, futures extinguished.

The people of both our countries are often told that cricket is the one thing that brings Indians and Australians together. That cricket is our single common denominator.

India's first Test series as a free country was played against Australia in November 1947, three months after our Independence. Yet the histories of our countries are linked together far more deeply than we think and further back in time than 1947.

We share something else other than cricket. Before they played the first Test match against each other, Indians and Australians fought wars together, on the same side. In Gallipoli, where, along with the thousands of Australians, over 1,300 Indians also lost their lives. In World War II, there were Indian and Australian soldiers in El Alamein, North Africa, in the Syria-Lebanon campaign, in Burma, in the battle for Singapore.

Before we were competitors, Indians and Australians were comrades. So it is only appropriate that we are here this evening at the Australian War Memorial, where along with celebrating cricket and cricketers, we remember the unknown soldiers of both nations.

It is however, incongruous, that I, an Indian, happen to be the first cricketer from outside Australia to be invited to deliver the Bradman Oration. I don't say that only because Sir Don once scored a hundred before lunch at Lord's and my 100 at Lord's this year took almost an entire day.

But more seriously, Sir Don played just five Tests against India; that was in the first India-Australia series in 1947–48, which was to be his last season at home. He didn't even play in India, and remains the most venerated cricketer in India not to have played there.

We know that he set foot in India though, in May 1953, when on his way to England to report on the Ashes for an English newspaper, his plane stopped in Calcutta airport. There were said to be close to a 1,000 people waiting to greet him; as you know, he was a very private person and so got into an army jeep and rushed into a barricaded building, annoyed with the airline for having 'breached confidentiality'. That was all Indians of the time saw of Bradman, who remains a mythical figure.

For one generation of fans in my country, those who grew up in the 1930s, when India was still under British rule, Bradman represented a cricketing excellence that belonged to somewhere outside England. To a country taking its first steps in Test cricket, that meant something. His success against England at that time was thought of as our personal success. He was striking one for all of us ruled by the common enemy. Or as your country has so poetically called them, the Poms.

There are two stories that I thought I should bring to your notice. On June 28, 1930, the day Bradman scored 254 at Lord's against England, was also the day Jawaharlal Nehru was arrested by the police. Nehru was, at the time, one of the most prominent leaders of the Indian Independence movement and later, independent India's first Prime Minister. The coincidence of the two events was noted by a young boy K.N. Prabhu, who was both nationalist, cricket fan and later became independent India's foremost cricket writer. In the '30s, as Nehru went in and out of jail, Bradman went after the England bowling and, for K.N. Prabhu, became a kind of avenging angel.

There's another story I've heard about the day in 1933, when the news reached India that Bradman's record for the highest Test score of 334 had been broken by Wally Hammond. As much as we love our records, they say some Indian fans at the time were not exactly happy. Now, there's a tale that a few even wanted to wear black bands to mourn the fact that this precious record that belonged to Australia—and by extension, us—had gone back. To an Englishman. We will never know if this is true, if black bands were ever worn, but as journalists sometimes tell me, why let facts get in the way of a good story.

My own link with Bradman was much like that of most other Indians—through history books, some old video footage and his wise words. About leaving the game better than you found it. About playing it positively, as Bradman, then a selector, told Richie Benaud before the 1960–61 West Indies tour of Australia. Of sending a right message out from cricket to its public. Of players being temporary trustees of a great game.

While there may be very little similarity in our records or our strike-rates or our fielding—and I can say this only today in front of all of you—I am actually pleased that I share something very important with Sir Don.

He was, primarily, like me, a No. 3 batsman. It is a tough, tough job.

We're the ones who make life easier for the kings of batting, the middle order that follows us. Bradman did that with a bit more success and style than I did. He dominated bowling attacks and put bums on seats, if I bat for any length of time I am more likely to bore people to sleep. Still, it is nice to have batted for a long time in a position, whose benchmark is, in fact, the benchmark for batsmanship itself.

Before he retired from public life in his eighties, I do know that Bradman watched Sunil Gavaskar's generation play a series in Australia. I remember the excitement that went through Indian cricket when we heard the news that Bradman had seen Sachin Tendulkar bat on TV and thought he batted like him. It was more than mere approval, it was as if the great Don had finally, passed on his torch. Not to an Aussie or an Englishman or a West Indian. But to one of our own.

One of the things Bradman said has stayed in my mind. That the finest of athletes had, along with skill, a few more essential qualities: to conduct their life with dignity, with integrity, with courage and modesty. All this he believed, were totally compatible with pride, ambition, determination and competitiveness. Maybe those words should be put up in cricket dressing rooms all over the world.

As all of you know, Don Bradman passed away on February 25, 2001, two days before the India v Australia series was to begin in Mumbai.

Whenever an important figure in cricket leaves us, cricket's global community pauses in the midst of contests and debates, to remember what he represented of us, what he stood for, and Bradman was the pinnacle. The standard against which all Test batsmen must take guard.

The series that followed two days after Bradman's death later went on to become what many believe was one of the greatest in cricket. It is a series, I'd like to believe, he would have enjoyed following.

A fierce contest between bat and ball went down to the final session of the final day of the final Test. Between an Australian team who had risen to their most imposing powers and a young Indian team determined to rewrite some chapters of its own history.

The 2001 series contained high-quality cricket from both sides and had a deep impact on the careers of those who played a part in it. The Australians were near unbeatable in the first half of the new decade, both home and away. As others floundered against them, India became the only team that competed with them on even terms.

India kept answering questions put to them by the Australians and asking a few themselves. The quality demanded of those contests, sometimes acrimonious, sometimes uplifting, made us, the Indian team, grow and rise. As individuals, we were asked to play to the absolute outer limits of our capabilities and we often extended them.

Now, whenever India and Australia meet, there is expectation and anticipation—and as we get into the next two months of the Border–Gavaskar Trophy, players on both sides will want to deliver their best.

When we toured in 2007–08, I thought it was going to be my last tour of Australia. The Australians thought it was going to be the last time they would be seeing Sachin Tendulkar on their shores. He received warm standing ovations from wonderful crowds all around the country.

Well, like a few, creaking Terminators, we're back. Older, wiser and I hope improved.

The Australian public will want to stand up to send Sachin off all over again this time. But I must warn you, given how he's been playing these days, there are no guarantees about final goodbyes.

In all seriousness, though, the cricket world is going to stop and watch Australia and India. It is Australia's first chance to defend their supremacy at home following defeat in the 2010 Ashes and a drawn series against New Zealand. It is India's opportunity to prove that the defeat to England in the summer was an aberration that we will bounce back from.

If both teams look back to their last 2007–08 series in Australia, they will know that they should have done things a little differently in the Sydney Test. But I think both sides have moved on from there; we've played each other twice in India already and relations between the two teams are much better than they have been as far as I can remember.

Thanks to the IPL, Indians and Australians have even shared dressing rooms. Shane

Watson's involvement in Rajasthan, Mike Hussey's role with Chennai to mention a few, are greatly appreciated back home. And even Shane Warne likes India now. I really enjoyed played alongside him at Rajasthan last season and can confidently report to you that he is not eating imported baked beans any more. In fact, looking at him, it seems, he is not eating anything.

It is often said that cricketers are ambassadors for their country; when there's a match to be won, sometimes we think that is an unreasonable demand. After all, what would career diplomats do if the result of a Test series depended on them, say, walking? But, as ties between India and Australia have strengthened and our contests have become more frequent, we realize that as Indian players, we stand for a vast, varied, often unfathomable and endlessly fascinating country.

At the moment, to much of the outside world, Indian cricket represents only two things—money and power. Yes, that aspect of Indian cricket is a part of the whole, but it is not the complete picture. As a player, as a proud and privileged member of the Indian cricket team, I want to say that, this one-dimensional, often cliched image relentlessly repeated is not what Indian cricket is really all about.

I cannot take all of you into the towns and villages our players come from, and introduce you to their families, teachers, coaches, mentors and team-mates who made them international cricketers. I cannot take all of you here to India to show you the belief, struggle, effort and sacrifice from hundreds of people that runs through our game.

As I stand here today, it is important for me to bring Indian cricket and its own remarkable story to you. I believe it is very necessary that cricketing nations try to find out about each other, try to understand each other and the different role cricket plays in different countries, because ours is, eventually, a very small world.

In India, cricket is a buzzing, humming, living entity going through a most remarkable time, like no other in our cricketing history.

In this last decade, the Indian team represents more than ever before, the country we come from—of people from vastly different cultures, who speak different languages, follow different religions, belong to all classes of society. I went around our dressing room to work out how many languages could be spoken in there and the number I have arrived at is: 15, including Shona and Afrikaans.

Most foreign captains, I think, would baulk at the idea. But, when I led India, I enjoyed it, I marvelled at the range of difference and the ability of people from so many different backgrounds to share a dressing room, to accept, accommodate and respect that difference. In a world growing more insular, that is a precious quality to acquire, because it stays for life and helps you understand people better, understand the significance of the other.

Let me tell you one of my favourite stories from my under-19 days, when the India under-19 team played a match against the New Zealand junior team. We had two bowlers in the team, one from the north Indian state of Uttar Pradesh—he spoke only Hindi, which is usually a link language for players from all over India, ahead even of English. It should have been alright, except the other bowler came from Kerala, in the deep south, and he spoke only the state's regional language, Malayalam. Now even that should have been okay as they were both bowlers and could bowl simultaneous spells.

Yet in one game, they happened to come together at the crease. In the dressing room, we were in splits, wondering how they were going to manage the business of a partnership, calling for runs or sharing the strike. Neither man could understand a word of what the other was saying and they were batting together. This could only happen in Indian cricket. Except that these two guys came up with a 100-run partnership. Their common language was cricket and that worked out just fine.

The everyday richness of Indian cricket lies right there, not in the news you hear about million-dollar deals and television rights.

When I look back over the twenty-five years I've spent in cricket, I realize two things. First, rather alarmingly, that I am the oldest man in the game, older to even Sachin by three months. More importantly, I realize that Indian cricket actually reflects our country's own growth story during this time. Cricket is so much a part of our national fabric that as India—its economy, society and popular culture—transformed itself, so did our most-loved sport.

As players we are appreciative beneficiaries of the financial strength of Indian cricket, but we are more than just mascots of that economic power. The caricature often made of Indian cricket and its cricketers in the rest of the world is that we are pampered superstars. Overpaid, underworked, treated like a cross between royalty and rock stars.

Yes, the Indian team has an enormous, emotional following and we do need security when we get around the country as a group. It is also why we make it a point to always try and conduct ourselves with composure and dignity.

On tour, I must point out, we don't attack fans or do drugs or get into drunken theatrics. And at home, despite what some of you may have heard, we don't live in mansions with swimming pools.

The news about the money may well overpower all else, but along with it, our cricket is full of stories the outside world does not see. Television rights generated around Indian cricket, are much talked about. Let me tell you what the television—around those much sought-after rights—has done to our game.

A sport that was largely played and patronized by princes and businessmen in traditional urban centres, cities like Bombay, Bangalore, Chennai, Baroda, Hyderabad, Delhi—has begun to pull in cricketers from everywhere.

As the earnings from Indian cricket have grown in the past two decades, mainly through television, the BCCI has spread revenues to various pockets in the country and improved where we play. The field is now spread wider than it ever has been, the ground covered by Indian cricket, has shifted.

Twenty seven teams compete in our national championship, the Ranji Trophy. Last season Rajasthan, a state best known for its palaces, fortresses and tourism won the Ranji Trophy title for the first time in its history. The national one-day championship also had a first-time winner in the newly formed state of Jharkhand, where our captain M.S. Dhoni comes from.

The growth and scale of cricket on our television was the engine of this population shift. Like Bradman was the boy from Bowral, a stream of Indian cricketers now come from what you could call India's outback.

Zaheer Khan belongs to the Maharashtra heartland, from a town that didn't have even one proper turf wicket. He could have been an instrumentation engineer but was drawn to cricket through TV and modelled his bowling by practicing in front of the mirror on his cupboard at home, and first bowled with a proper cricket ball at the age of 17.

One day out of nowhere, a boy from a village in Gujarat turned up as India's fastest bowler.

After Munaf Patel made his debut for India, the road from the nearest railway station to his village had to be improved because journalists and TV crews from the cities kept landing up there.

We are delighted that Umesh Yadav didn't become a policeman like he was planning and turned to cricket instead. He is the first cricketer from the central Indian first-class team of Vidarbha to play Test cricket.

Virender Sehwag, it shouldn't surprise you, belongs to the wild west just outside Delhi. He had been enrolled in a college which had a good cricket programme and travelled 84 kms every day by bus to get to practice and matches.

Every player in this room wearing an India blazer has a story like this. Here, ladies and gentlemen, is the heart and soul of Indian cricket.

Playing for India completely changes our lives. The game has given us a chance to pay back our debt to all those who gave their time, energy and resources for us to be better cricketers: we can build new homes for our parents, get our siblings married off in style, give our families very comfortable lives.

The Indian cricket team is in fact, India itself, in microcosm. A sport that was played first by princes, then their subordinates, then the urban elite, is now a sport played by all of India. Cricket, as my two under-19 team-mates proved, is India's most widely spoken language. Even Indian cinema has its regional favourites; a movie star in the south may not be popular in the north. But a cricketer? Loved everywhere.

It is also a very tough environment to grow up in—criticism can be severe, responses to victory and defeat extreme. There are invasions of privacy and stones have been thrown at our homes after some defeats.

It takes time getting used to, extreme reactions can fill us with anger. But every cricketer realizes at some stage of his career, that the Indian cricket fan is best understood by remembering the sentiment of the majority, not the actions of a minority.

One of the things that has always lifted me

as a player is looking out of the team bus when we travelled somewhere in India. When people see the Indian bus going by, see some of us sitting with our curtains drawn back, it always amazes me how much they light up. There is an instantaneous smile, directed not just at the player they see—but at the game we play that, for whatever reason, means something to people's lives. Win or lose, the man on the street will smile and give you a wave.

After India won the World Cup this year, our players were not congratulated as much as they were thanked by people they ran into. 'You have given us everything,' they were told, 'all of us have won.' Cricket in India now stands not just for sport, but possibility, hope, opportunities.

On our way to the Indian team, we know of so many of our team-mates, some of whom may have been equally or more talented than those sitting here, who missed out. When I started out, for a young Indian, cricket was the ultimate gamble—all or nothing, no safety nets. No second chances for those without an education or a college degree or second careers. Indian cricket's wealth now means a wider pool of well-paid cricketers even at first-class level.

For those of us who make it to the Indian team, cricket is not merely our livelihood, it is a gift we have been given. Without the game, we would just be average people leading average lives. As Indian cricketers, our sport has given us the chance do something worthwhile with our lives. How many people could say that?

This is the time Indian cricket should be flowering; we are the world champions in the short game, and over the space of the next twelve months should be involved in a tight contest with Australia, South Africa and England to determine which one of us is the world's strongest Test team.

Yet I believe this is also a time for introspection within our game, not only in India, but all over the world. We have been given some alerts and responding to them quickly is the smart thing to do.

I was surprised a few months ago to see the lack of crowds in an ODI series featuring India. By that I don't mean the lack of full houses, I think it was the sight of empty stands I found somewhat alarming.

India played its first one-day international at home in November 1981, when I was nine. Between then and now India have played 227 ODIs at home; the October five-match series against England was the first time that the grounds have not been full for an ODI featuring the Indian team.

In the summer of 1998, I played in a one-dayer against Kenya in Kolkata and the Eden Gardens was full. Our next game was held in the 48-degree heat of Gwalior and the stands were heaving.

The October series against England was the first one at home after India's World Cup win. It was called the 'revenge' series meant to wipe away the memory of a forgettable tour of England. India kept winning every game, and yet the stands did not fill up. Five days after a 5-0 victory 95,000 turned up to watch the India's first Formula One race.

A few weeks later I played in a Test match against West Indies in Calcutta, in front of what was the lowest turnout in Eden Gardens' history. Yes we still wanted to win and our intensity did not dip. But at the end of the day, we are performers, entertainers and we love an audience. The audience amplifies everything you are doing, the bigger the crowd the bigger the occasion, its magnitude, its emotion. When I think about the Eden Gardens crowds this year, I wonder what the famous Calcutta Test of 2001 would have felt like with 50,000 people less watching us.

Australia and South Africa played an exciting and thrilling Test series recently and two great Test matches produced some fantastic performances from players of both teams, but were sadly played in front of sparse crowds.

It is not the numbers that Test players need, it is the atmosphere of a Test that every player wants to revel in and draw energy from. My first reaction to the lack of crowds for cricket was that there had been a lot of cricket and so perhaps, a certain amount of spectator-fatigue. That is too simplistic a view; it's the easy thing to say but might not be the only thing.

The India vs England ODI series had no context, because the two countries had played each other in four Tests and five ODIs just a few weeks before. When India and West Indies played ODIs a month after that the grounds were full, but this time the matches were played in smaller venues that didn't host too much international cricket. Maybe our clues are all there and we must remain vigilant.

Unlike Australia or England, Indian cricket has never had to compete with other sports for a share of revenues, mind space or crowd attendance at international matches. The lack of crowds may not directly impact on revenues or how important the sport is to Indians, but we do need to accept that there has definitely been a change in temperature over, I think, the last two years.

Whatever the reasons are—maybe it is too much cricket or too little by way of comfort for spectators—the fan has sent us a message and we must listen. This is not mere sentimentality. Empty stands do not make for good television. Bad television can lead to a fall in ratings, the fall in ratings will be felt by media planners and advertisers looking elsewhere.

If that happens, it is hard to see television rights around cricket being as sought after as they have always been in the last fifteen years. And where does that leave everyone? I'm not trying to be an economist or doomsday prophet—this is just how I see it.

Let us not be so satisfied with the present, with deals and finances in hand that we get blindsided. Everything that has given cricket its power and influence in the world of sports has started from that fan in the stadium. They deserve our respect and let us not take them for granted. Disrespecting fans is disrespecting the game. The fans have stood by our game through everything. When we play, we need to think of them. As players, the balance between competitiveness and fairness can be tough but it must be found.

If we stand up for the game's basic decencies, it will be far easier to tackle its bigger dangers—whether it is finding short cuts to easy money or being lured by the scourge of spot-fixing and contemplating any involvement with the betting industry.

Cricket's financial success means it will face threats from outside the game and keep facing them. The last two decades have proved this over and over again. The internet and modern technology may just end up being a step ahead of every anti-corruption regulation in place in the game. As players, the one way we can stay ahead for the game, is if we are willing to be monitored and regulated closely.

Even if it means giving up a little bit of freedom of movement and privacy. If it means undergoing dope tests, let us never say no. If it means undergoing lie-detector tests, let us understand the technology, what purpose it serves and accept it. Now lie-detectors are by no means perfect but they could actually help the innocent clear their names. Similarly, we should not object to having our finances scrutinized if that is what is required.

When the first anti-corruption measures were put into place, we did moan a little bit about being accredited and depositing our cell phones with the manager. But now we must treat it like we do airport security because we know it is for our own good and our own security.

Players should be ready to give up a little personal space and personal comfort for this game, which has given us so much. If you have nothing to hide, you have nothing to fear.

Other sports have borrowed from cricket's anti-corruption measures to set up their own ethical governance programmes and we must take pride in belonging to a sport that is professional and progressive.

...Because the game is bigger than us all, we must think way ahead of how it stands today. Where do we want it to be in the year 2020? Or say in 2027, when it will be 150 years since the first Test match was played. If you think about it, cricket has been with us longer than the modern motor car, it existed before modern air travel took off.

As much as cricket's revenues are important to its growth, its traditions and its vibrancy are a necessary part of its progress in the future. We shouldn't let either go because we played too much of one format and too little of the other.

Professionalism has given cricketers of my generation privileged lives and we know it, even though you may often hear us whining about burn-out, travel and the lack of recovery time.

Whenever we begin to get into that mindset, it's good to remember a piece of Sachin's conversation with Bradman. Sachin told us that he had asked Sir Don how he had mentally prepared for big games, what his routines were. Sir Don said that, well, before a game he would go to work and after the game go back to work. Whenever a cricketer feels a whinge coming on, that would be good to remember.

Before I conclude, I also want to talk briefly about an experience I have often had over the course of my career. It is not to do with individuals or incidents, but one I believe is important to share. I have sometimes found myself in the middle of a big game, standing at slip or even at the non-strikers end and suddenly realized that everything else has vanished. At that moment, all that exists is the contest and the very real sense of the joy that comes from playing the game.

It is an almost meditative experience, where you reconnect with the game just like you did years ago, when you first began, when you hit your first boundary, took the first catch, scored your first century, or were involved in a big victory. It lasts for a very fleeting passage of time, but it is a very precious instant and every cricketer should hang on to it.

I know it is utterly fanciful to expect professional cricketers to play the game like amateurs; but the trick, I believe, is taking the spirit of the amateur—of discovery, of learning, of pure joy, of playing by the rules—into our profession. Taking it to practice or play, even when there's an epidemic of white-line fever breaking out all over the field.

In every cricketer there lies a competitor who hates losing, and yes, winning matters. But it is not the only thing that matters when you play cricket. How it is played is as important for every member of every team because every game we play leaves a footprint in cricket's history. We must never forget that.

What we do as professionals is easily carried over into the amateur game, in every way—batting, bowling, fielding, appealing, celebration, dissent, argument. In the players of 2027, we will see a reflection of this time and of ourselves and it had better not annoy or anguish us fifty year olds.

As the game's custodians, it is important we are not tempted by the short-term gains of the backward step. We can be remembered for being the generation that could take the giant stride.

Thank you for the invitation to address all of you tonight, and your attention.

## AZIM PREMJI

### Thoughts on Philanthropy

*New Delhi, 2013*

*Azim Hashim Premji (b. 1945) is an Indian business leader and a leading philanthropist. He is Chariman of the Wipro group of companies and has overseen its growth as one of India's biggest IT companies. He started the Azim Premji Foundation with a $2.2 billion donation. The foundation is focused on education at all levels. He delivered this speech at the Economic Times Award, December 2013.*

Good evening. It's a pleasure to be here with all of you. I want to thank the *Economic Times* for bestowing this honor on me. While I receive this honor, the simple fact is that it is actually an honour for the thousands of my colleagues and partners, who have helped build Wipro into what it is, over the past few decades. Thank you. It was suggested by the *Economic Times* that I share some thoughts on philanthropy on this occasion. So let me do so.

Let's think about tonight. We will all go home or go to our hotels and sleep. No matter where we are, within a couple of kilometers of where we are sleeping safely and soundly, there will be a young girl, who is our daughter's age or our granddaughter's age, trying to sleep in the cold night of December on the roads. She has been abused in the past, and she will be abused in the future. She is probably desperately hungry. In her circumstances, going to school or having anything else that every child must have, is not even a remote possibility. When she wakes up tomorrow morning, it's just the start of another day of trying to survive, to again sleep shivering on the cold pavement somewhere. This girl is not alone. There are probably 3 million children, who are homeless and will sleep on the streets in India tonight and every night. She is also not alone in sleeping hungry. More than

200 million of our people will probably sleep hungry, like her. In very simple terms: can we be indifferent to this?

To my mind that is the basic question that we need to ask ourselves, do we feel connected to our country, to the people around us? Should not every Indian have the very basic, very bare necessities of a life of dignity? This is certainly not hoping for too much, it's just basic safety, adequate food, a roof to sleep, basic education and healthcare. Most of us would feel this way. I think we just need to act. I have mentioned only a few kinds of issues. But as all of us know, our country is facing challenges of similar kind on every front. Be it education, healthcare, nutrition, sanitation or of deep inequality and discrimination. Each one is as complex as the other, and each one as necessary for a life of basic dignity. We can perhaps justifiably say that many of these issues need to be addressed by the government. Certainly the government needs to do more and better. But that doesn't in any way lessen the responsibility that we have. I and you, who have the privilege of being successful, have a greater responsibility. To me, philanthropy is the connection that we can have if we are not indifferent to all these issues that face us. It is the mechanism for us to contribute to making some positive change. And I think greater our success, the greater the responsibility for us. I must also say that the desire to engage must come from within. No one can be told to be philanthropic.

At its core philanthropy is about the connection that you feel with the people around you or the world around you. Many who feel this connection and have taken action, have experienced that there is enough reason for hope in our country, and that one can genuinely contribute. The foundation that we have set up has been working with various state governments to improve equity and quality of government schools for the past twelve years. I have learnt that trying to improve education is a very long process, but I think that basic education is the basic route to building a better society, so we remain totally committed to it.

Let me narrate one of many things that give us hope in this journey. We work in some of the most disadvantaged districts of the country. We have fifty to seventy of our own people in each of these districts. They are all deeply committed to the cause of education, and are capable of educating teachers. In all these places we run voluntary learning forums for government school teachers, amongst many other initiatives. What this means is that teachers come to these learning sessions on their own. They spend their own money for transportation; they come from up to 30 km away in difficult conditions. They also spend their own money on food. They do this on a holiday, usually a Sunday. Can we imagine this happening in the best of companies? How many employees of such companies will spend their holidays and their own money, so that they can do their jobs better? How completely contrary is this experience of ours, to the notion of the disinterested government employee? These are all government employees, but they are deeply committed and they genuinely care. Our experience has been that between 12-18 per cent teachers in a district become a part of such forums over a period of time. And if you ask them why they do it, they all have the same answer, which is that they want to learn so that they can teach better. We are not talking about small numbers. In a typical district with 5000 teachers, this implies that 600-800 teachers are engaged in such forums. I find this a great reason for hope. When so many people from within the government school system have this kind of commitment, I am sure education will improve, given time and sustained effort.

As I said before we have been at it for twelve years. I have only one regret about my philanthropy, which is that, I wish I had started earlier. There is so much to do, and this kind of work takes so much time that the earlier we try to contribute, the better it is. With these twelve years of our experience, let me share three other things that I have learnt about philanthropy. Those of you who are very active in philanthropy would perhaps resonate with these lessons that I have learnt.

First, involving your family early on in philanthropy is very important. Their understanding, endorsement and involvement may eventually be the most determining factor. There is another positive aspect to this early involvement. Some of the smartest people that I know have been those who chose to become homemakers. They can perhaps play a significant role in starting off their families' philanthropic efforts.

Second, the key to scaling up philanthropy and doing good work is getting good people in the team. This is exactly the same as in our businesses. The work in philanthropy is perhaps more complex than business, because social issues are more complex. So it needs really good people. I think that the most serious start to anyone's philanthropic work would be to pick one of their top people from within the business, a person who has the intent, empathy, ability, and trust and move him or her to the philanthropy side.

Third, philanthropic work needs patience, tenacity and empathy. It is different from business. We all know that intellectually, but it's very challenging when one gets in to it. One has to change one's mindset significantly, if one has to make a difference. I have learnt this only slowly in the past twelve years.

Thank you for hearing me out. I absolutely believe that we are trustees of our wealth for this society, and we must use it as such. We must do philanthropy because it is the right thing to do. I also believe that every one of us has the basic empathy with the people around us; we just need to let it find expression. I am certain that none of us wants to let the young girl I talked about earlier to go hungry, to get abused, or to sleep in the cold night of December on the road, when our daughters and granddaughters are sleeping safe and sound—as they should. Thank you.

## SHASHI THAROOR

An Era of Darkness

*Oxford, 2015*

*Shashi Tharoor (b. 1956) is a politician who has also been a career diplomat. He is a Member of Parliament in the Lok Sabha and was an official at the United Nations till 2007, where he rose to the rank of Under Secretary-General for Communications and Public Information. He is also an acclaimed writer and has written a number of works of fiction and non-fiction. Shashi Tharoor is known for his powerful oratory and eloquence. He gave the following speech as an Oxford Union Debate argument in July 2015, speaking for the motion: Britain Owes Repatriations to Its Former Colonies. The video of this speech went viral online and has gathered over 4.9 million views.*

Madam President and gentlemen, ladies of the house,

I, standing here with eight minutes in my hands at this venerable and rather magnificent institution, I was going to assure you that I belong to the Henry VIII school of public speaking—that as Henry VIII said to his wives, 'I shall not keep you long.' But now finding myself the seventh speaker out of eight in what must already seem a rather long evening to you, I rather feel like Henry VIII's last wife. I know more or less what is expected of me but I am not sure how to do it any differently.

Perhaps what I should do is really try and pay attention to the arguments that have been advanced by the Opposition today. We had for example Sir Richard Ottaway suggesting—challenging the very idea that it could be argued that the economic situation of the colonies was actually worsened by the experience of British colonialism.

Well I stand to offer you the Indian example, Sir Richard. India's share of the world economy when Britain arrived on its shores was 23 per cent, by the time the British left it was down to below 4 per cent. Why? Simply because India had been governed for the benefit of Britain.

Britain's rise for 200 years was financed by its depredations in India. In fact, Britain's industrial revolution was actually premised upon the de-industrialization of India.

The handloom weavers, for example, famed across the world, whose products were exported around the world. These weavers were making fine muslin as light as woven air, it was said, and Britain came right in, smashed their thumbs, broke their looms, imposed tariffs and duties on their cloth and products and started, of course, taking their raw material from India and shipping back manufactured cloth, flooding the world's markets with what became the products of the dark and satanic mills of Victorian England.

That meant that the weavers in India became beggars and India went from being a world-famous exporter of finished cloth into an importer; went from having 27 per cent of the world's trade to less than 2 per cent.

Meanwhile, colonialists like Robert Clive bought their rotten boroughs in England on the proceeds of their loot in India while taking the Hindi word 'loot' into their dictionaries as well as their habits.

And the British had the gall to call him Clive of India as if he belonged to the country, when all he really did was to ensure that much of the country belonged to him.

By the end of nineteenth century, the fact is that India was already Britain's biggest cash cow, the world's biggest purchaser of British goods and exports and the source of highly paid employment for British civil servants. We literally paid for our own oppression. And as has been pointed out, the wealthy Victorian British families that made their money out of the slave economy—one-fifth of the elites of the wealthy class in Britain in nineteenth century owed their money to transporting 3 million Africans across the waters. In 1833, when slavery was abolished, a compensation of 20 million pounds was paid not as reparations to those who had lost their lives or who had suffered or been oppressed by slavery but to those who had lost their property.

I was struck by the fact that your Wi-Fi password at this Union commemorates the name of Mr Gladstone—the great liberal hero. Well, I am sorry his family was one of those who benefited from this compensation.

Staying with India. Between 15 and 29 million Indians died of starvation in British-induced famines. The most famous example was, of course, the great Bengal famine during World War II when 4 million people died because Winston Churchill deliberately, as a matter of written policy, proceeded to divert essential supplies from civilians in Bengal to sturdy tummies and Europeans as reserve stockpiles.

He said that the starvation of anyway underfed Bengalis mattered much less than that of sturdy Greeks—Churchill's actual quote. And when conscience-stricken British officials wrote to him pointing out that people were dying because of this decision, he peevishly wrote in the margins of the file, 'Why hasn't Gandhi died yet?'

So, all notions that the British were trying to do their colonial enterprise out of enlightened despotism to try and bring the benefits of colonialism and civilization to the benighted heathen, I am sorry—Churchill's conduct in 1943 is simply one example of many that give the lie to this myth.

As others have said on the proposition—violence and racism were the reality of the colonial experience. And no wonder that the sun never set on the British empire because even god couldn't trust the English in the dark.

Let me take World War I as a very concrete example since the first speaker Mr Lee suggested these things couldn't be quantified. Well, let me quantify World War I for you. Again, I am sorry, from an Indian perspective, [as] others have spoken of other countries. One-sixth of all the British forces that fought in the war were Indian—54,000 Indians actually lost their lives in that war, 65,000 were wounded and another 4,000 remained missing or in prison.

Indian taxpayers had to cough up a hundred million pounds in that time's money. India supplied 17 million rounds of ammunition, 6,00,000 rifles and machine guns, 42 million garments were stitched and sent out of India and 1.3 million Indian personnel served in this war. I know all this because the commemoration of the centenary has just taken place.

But not just that, India had to supply 1,73,000 animals, 370 million tonnes of supplies and in the end the total value of everything that was taken out of India, and India by the way was suffering from recession at that time and poverty and hunger, was in today's money 8 billion pounds. You want quantification, it's available.

World War II, it was even worse—2.5 million Indians in uniform. I won't belabour the point but of Britain's total war debt of 3 billion pounds in 1945 money, 1.25 billion was owed to India and never actually paid.

Somebody mentioned Scotland, well the

fact is that colonialism actually cemented your union with Scotland. The Scots had tried to send colonies out before 1707, they had all failed, I am sorry to say. But, then of course, came union and India was available and there you had a disproportionate employment of Scots—I am sorry Mr Mckinsey has to speak after me—engaged in this colonial enterprise as soldiers, as merchants, as agents, as employees and their earnings from India is what brought prosperity to Scotland, even pulled Scotland out of poverty. Now that India is no longer there, no wonder the bonds are loosening.

Now we have heard other arguments on this side and there has been a mention of railways. Well let me tell you first of all as my colleague the Jamaican High Commissioner has pointed out, the railways and roads were really built to serve British interests and not those of the local people but I might add that many countries have built railways and roads without having had to be colonized in order to do so.

They were designed to carry raw materials

from the hinterland into the ports to be shipped to Britain. And the fact is that the Indian or Jamaican or other colonial public—their needs were incidental. Transportation: there was no attempt made to match supply to demand. Instead in fact the Indian railways were built with massive incentives offered by Britain to British investors, guaranteed out of Indian taxes paid by Indians with the result that you actually had one mile of Indian railway costing twice what it cost to build the same mile in Canada or Australia because there was so much money being paid in extravagant returns.

Britain made all the profits, controlled the technology, supplied all the equipment and absolutely all these benefits came as British private enterprise at Indian public risk. That was the railways as an accomplishment.

We are hearing about aid, I think it was Sir Richard Ottaway who mentioned British aid to India. Well let me just point out that the British aid to India is about 0.4 per cent of India's GDP. The government of India actually spends more on fertilizer subsidies which might be an appropriate metaphor for that argument.

If I may point out as well that as my fellow speakers from the proposition have pointed out, there have been incidents of racial violence, of loot, of massacres, of bloodshed, of transportation in India's case even one of our last Mughal emperors. Yes, maybe today's Britains are not responsible for some of these reparations but the same speakers have pointed with pride to their foreign aid—you are not responsible for the people starving in Somalia but you give them aid—surely the principle of reparations for the wrongs that have been done cannot be denied.

It's been pointed out, for example, dehumanization of Africans in the Caribbean, the massive psychological damage that has been done, the undermining of social traditions, of property rights, of the authority structures of these societies—all in the interest of British colonialism and the fact remains that many of today's problems in these countries including the persistence and in some cases the creation of racial and ethnic and religious tensions were the direct result of the colonial experience. So there is a moral debt that needs to be paid.

Someone challenged reparations elsewhere. Well I am sorry Germany doesn't just give reparations to Israel, it also gives reparations to Poland. Perhaps some of the speakers here are too young to remember the dramatic picture of Chancellor Willy Brandt on his knees in the Warsaw Ghetto in 1970.

There are other examples, there is Italy's reparations to Libya, there is Japan's to Korea even Britain has paid reparations to the New Zealand Maoris. So it is not as if this is something that is unprecedented or unheard of that somehow opens some sort of nasty Pandora's box.

No wonder Professor Louis reminded us that he is from Texas. There is a wonderful expression in Texas that summarises the arguments of the opposition 'All hat and no cattle'.

Now, if I can just quickly look through the

other notes that I was scribbling while they were speaking, there was a reference to democracy and rule of law. Let me say with the greatest possible respect, you cannot oppress, enslave, kill, maim, torture people for 200 years and then celebrate the fact that they are democratic at the end of it!

We were denied democracy so we had to snatch it, seize it from you. With the greatest of reluctance it was conceded in India's case after 150 years of British rule and that too with limited franchise.

If I may just point out the arguments made by a couple of speakers. The first speaker Mr Lee in particular conceded all the evil atrocities of colonialism but essentially suggested that reparations won't really help, they won't help the right people, they would be used a propaganda tool, they will embolden people like Mr Mugabe. It's nice how in the old days, I am sorry to say, that the people of the Caribbean used to frighten their children into behaving and sleeping by saying Sir Francis

Drake would come after them—that was the legacy. Now Mugabe will be there—the new sort of Sir Francis Drake of our time.

The fact is, very simply sir, that we are not talking about reparations as a tool to empower anybody, they are a tool for you to atone, for the wrongs that have been done and I am quite prepared to accept the proposition that you can't evaluate, put a monetary sum on the kinds of horrors people have suffered. Certainly no amount of money can expiate the loss of a loved one as somebody pointed out there. You are not going to figure out the exact amount but the principle is what matters.

The fact is that to speak blithely of sacrifices on both sides as an analogy was used here—a burglar comes into your house, ransacks the place, stubs his toe and you say, well, there was sacrifice on both sides—that is not an acceptable argument. The truth is that we are not arguing specifically that vast sums of money need to be paid. The proposition before this house is the principle of owing reparations, not the fine points of how much is owed, to whom it should be paid. The question is, is there a debt, does Britain owe reparations?

As far as I am concerned, the ability to acknowledge a wrong that has been done, to simply say sorry will go a far far far longer way than some percentage of GDP in the form of aid.

What is required it seems to me is accepting the principle that reparations are owed. Personally, I'd be quite happy if it was one pound a year for the next 200 years after the last 200 years of Britain in India.

Thank you very much Madam President.

## RUSKIN BOND

### When Books Become Friends

*Dehradun, 2015*

*Ruskin Bond (b. 1934) is the author of a number of novels, short stories, essays and poetry. He is one of India's most-loved children's writers. He was awarded the Padma Shri in 1999 and the Padma Bhushan in 2014. This is an edited version of a speech delivered during an interaction with school children in Dehradun in the winter of 2015.*

I am no good at giving speeches or delivering lectures. When I was young, I used to resent being lectured to, and I would usually fall asleep—sometimes with my eyes open! I would rather have conversations than make speeches, especially with young friends like you.

So this will be a very short speech. And I will

talk about friendship. We all need friends, but some of us have difficulty making friends with our classmates and neighbours, or even at home. For some years as a small boy, I found myself in a similar situation, and this was when I began a lifelong friendship with books.

I was a lonely child. Loneliness is not something you invite, it is imposed on you by circumstance. In my case it was the death of my dear father when I was ten. My parents had separated some years earlier and I lived alone with my father in Delhi, where he was working with the Royal Air Force. He spent all his mornings and evenings with me, when he was not at work, and on weekends he would take me to the pictures or restaurants in Connaught Place or for walks to the parks and monuments nearby. He would also take me to a bookshop in Connaught Place where I would buy my favourite comics.

This was how I began reading. My father also bought me books—I remember *Alice in Wonderland* and the Biggles books, featuring the daredevil pilot James Bigglesworth, whose adventures I enjoyed more than Alice's! I would spend the day reading my comics and books and listening to records on our gramophone, until my father came back from work and then he would give me all his time and attention. He was my best friend, and he pampered me, so that when I lost him, I thought I had lost the only person in the world who loved me unconditionally.

So I was lonely after him. It took me some time to adjust to my changed circumstances and my new family. My mother had remarried. I had very few close friends in my boarding school, Bishop Cottons in Shimla. This was when I found what good friends books can be.

My mother and stepfather were not great readers, there were no books at home. But they enjoyed going on shikar expeditions, and on one occasion, they took me with them—I had come to spend the winter vacations with them in Dehradun. I did not join them for the shikar and stayed behind in the forest rest house. It was near Timli Pass, some you may have heard of it. I was wandering around the large rest house when, lo and behold, I discovered a dusty but crowded bookshelf! It was almost hidden in a corner of the back verandah. I wiped the dust off the covers and examined the titles. My reading taste had not yet formed, so I was ready to try anything. I read like a thirsty man drinks water! The bookshelf had a variety of books—and my own interest in books has remained equally wide-ranging.

Over three days in that forest rest house, I read P.G. Wodehouse, Agatha Christie, M.R. James—who wrote ghost stories—*The Diary of a Nobody*, a very funny book by George and Weedon Grossmith, *The Big Karoo* by a South African writer called Pauline Smith, and *David Copperfield*, which influenced me—I wanted to run away like David Copperfield and become a writer!

The shikaris did not manage to hunt anything, but I had found a treasure in the forest. I hadn't been lonely or bored in all my three days in the rest house.

Shortly after that, a kind school master put me in charge of the library in my boarding school. I had the key to the library, and that changed my life. I could make friends with so many writers and the characters they had created. Over a year and a half I read Dickens, Stevenson, Jack London, H.G. Wells, the Bronte sisters, Maugham, Mark Twain, Jerome K. Jerome and so many others. I could travel across the world with them and discover different kinds of people, many of them in circumstances similar to mine. I could also escape from morning PT and compulsory sports and running—you know, those horrors you have in boarding school. I would just lock myself up in the library and have a good time.

Later, when I went abroad at seventeen, I suffered so much from homesickness for India that I made myself ill and ended up in a London hospital with jaundice and an eye disease. It took me a month to be up and about again, but it would have taken much longer if a kind friend hadn't brought me a bunch of books which he thought might cheer me up. One of these was by an Indian writer, Sudhin Ghose, called *And Gazelles Leaping*, about a boy growing up in rural Bengal. Another was called *Rungli Rungliot*, a journal kept by the famous English writer Rumer Godden of her time in a beautiful tea garden near Darjeeling. Reading these books, I was determined to get well and return to India.

Even today, I can lose myself in a book and forget the troubles and irritations that visit all of us sometimes. When you are down or feel discouraged or alone, pick up a book. These days you have your computers and smartphones. You can read on those too, but a printed book comes with the advantage of the feel and smell of paper. It makes reading an intimate experience. And you can put a flower or a leaf between the pages, or a letter from a friend you love.

I have been lucky that I fell in love with books when I was very young. I wish that love and companionship for all of you.

## RAGHURAM RAJAN

### The Spirit of Enquiry

*New Delhi, 2015*

*Raghuram Rajan (b. 1963) is an economist and academic. He was the twenty-third Governor of the Reserve Bank of India from 2013 to 2016. He is also the author of a number of books on economics. This speech was delivered at the Convocation at the Indian Institute of Technology, Delhi, in October 2015, where he spoke about the need for debate and enquiry, and how it is important for economic growth.*

Thank you very much for inviting me back to the Institute to deliver the convocation address. I graduated with a degree in Electrical Engineering thirty years ago. I was overly anxious then about what the future held for me, because I did not realize that the Institute had prepared me so well for what lay ahead. Our professors—and I will not single out any to avoid a disservice to those I do not name—were dedicated professionals. They asked a lot of us, knowing that in challenging us they allowed us to learn what we were capable of. Equally important, our Electrical Engineering class—in those days, Computer Science was part of Electrical Engineering in IIT Delhi—had some of the smartest people it has been my privilege to know. After working with them as colleagues, and competing with them for grades, I learned what it took to succeed in the fiercest environments; very hard work, friendship, and boatloads of luck. Those lessons have stayed with me since.

IIT Delhi then, as I am sure it is now, was not only about studies—it was about growing up. We were, with a few notable exceptions, the proverbial school nerds who had been excluded from all school sports by the macho sports cases. With almost everyone in the same boat at

IIT, for the first time in our lives we got a chance to bat and bowl at the nets, instead of being posted at deep long on to retrieve the odd six by the stars. Everyone did something, ranging from photography to publishing. Of course, we all aspired to join dramatics, where you got to spend long hours with members of the opposite sex. Unfortunately, I was no good at acting, so I had to look for self-actualisation elsewhere. But there were enough places to look.

Student politics was vibrant, with plenty of scheming, strategizing and back-stabbing. It was an intellectual pastime, however, without the violence and corruption that plagues student politics elsewhere in our country. You had to convince the small intelligent electorate to vote for you, and in figuring out how to get that vote, we all learnt the art of persuasion.

So we grew up in the classrooms, in the squash courts at the RCA, in the civilizing SPIC MACAY [Society for the Promotion of Indian Classical Music And Culture Amongst Youth] overnight classical music concerts and in the over-crowded rock concerts at the OAT. Some of us spent long hours waiting hopefully outside Kailash Hostel, and when occasionally our wait was rewarded, beautiful autumn nights with our friends, chatting and gazing at the stars while sitting on the roof of Convocation Hall. The Institute replaced our naivety with a more confident maturity. We came in as smart boys and girls and left as wiser young men and women. I am confident that the Institute has done to you what it did to us. You will thank it in the years to come for that.

In speaking here today, I am aware that most convocation addresses are soon forgotten. That creates a form of moral hazard for the speaker. If you are not going to remember what I say, I don't have the incentive to work hard at crafting my words. The net effect is what economists refer to as a bad equilibrium; my speech is forgettable, and you therefore forget it soon. If so, we are all probably better off with me skipping the rest of the speech, and all of us going on to other pressing duties.

Nevertheless, I am going to look beyond my personal incentives and fulfil my dharma as Chief Guest. I will speak on why India's tradition of debate and an open spirit of enquiry is critical for its economic progress. Let me explain.

Robert Solow won the Nobel Prize in Economics for work that showed that the bulk of economic growth did not come from putting more factors of production such as labour and capital to work. Instead, it came from putting those factors of production together more cleverly, that is, from what he called total factor productivity growth. Put differently, new ideas, new methods of production, better logistics—these are what lead to sustained economic growth. Of course, a poor country like ours can grow for some time by putting more people to work, by moving them from low productivity agriculture to higher value-added industry or services, and by giving them better tools to do their jobs. As many of you who have taken economics will recognize, we in India are usually far from the production possibility frontier, so we can grow for a long while just by catching up with the methods of industrial countries.

But more intelligent ways of working will enable us to leapfrog old methods and come more quickly to the production possibility frontier—as for example we have done in parts of the software industry. And, of course, once you are at the frontier and using the best methods in the world, the only way to grow is to innovate and be even better than others in the world. This is what our software firms are now trying to do.

Our alums, whom you students will shortly join, are leading India's charge to the frontier and beyond. Take the fantastic developments in E-commerce, ranging from the creation of electronic marketplaces to new logistics networks and payments systems. Today, a consumer in a small town can have the same choice of clothing fashions that anyone from the large metros enjoy, simply because the Internet has brought all the shops in India to her doorstep. And while her local shop no longer can sell shoddy apparel, it now focuses on the perishable items she needs in a hurry, even while sub-contracting to provide the last leg of the logistic network that reaches her. Economic growth through new ideas and production methods is what our professors and alums contribute to the nation.

So what does an educational institution or a nation need to do to keep the idea factory open? The first essential is to foster competition in the market place for ideas. This means encouraging challenge to all authority and tradition, even while acknowledging that the only way of dismissing any view is through empirical tests. What this rules out is anyone imposing a particular view or ideology because of their power. Instead, all ideas should be scrutinized critically, no matter whether they originate domestically or abroad, whether they have matured over thousands of years or a few minutes, whether they come from an untutored student or a world-famous professor.

I am sure many of you have come across Richard Feynman's Lectures on Physics, a must-read when we were at IIT. The Nobel prize-winning physicist was one of the giants of the twentieth century. In his autobiography, though, he writes how he found the atmosphere at the Institute of Advanced Studies at Princeton stultifying. Now, as you know, the Institute of Advanced Studies brings together some of the finest scholars in the world to ponder problems in a multi-disciplinary environment. But he found the atmosphere sterile because there were no students to ask him questions, questions that would force him to rethink his beliefs and perhaps discover new theories. Ideas start with questioning and alternative viewpoints, sometimes seemingly silly ones. After all, Einstein built his theory of relativity pondering the somewhat wacky question of what someone travelling in a train at the speed of light would experience. So nothing should be excluded but everything should be subject to debate and constant testing. No one should be allowed to offer unquestioned pronouncements. Without this competition for ideas, we have stagnation.

This then leads to a second essential: Protection, not of specific ideas and traditions, but the right to question and challenge, the right to behave differently so long as it does not hurt others seriously. In this protection lies societal self-interest, for it is by encouraging the challenge of innovative rebels that society develops, that it gets the ideas that propel Solow's total factor productivity growth. Fortunately, India has always protected debate and the right to have different views. Some have even embedded these views in permanent structures. Raja Raja Chola, in building the magnificent Brihadeeswara Shaivite temple at Thanjavur, also incorporated sculptures of Vishnu as well as the meditating Buddha thus admitting to alternative viewpoints. When Shahenshah Jalaluddin Muhammad Akbar invited scholars of all manner of persuasion to debate the eternal verities at his court, he was only following older traditions of our Hindu and Buddhist kings, who encouraged and protected the spirit of enquiry.

What then of group sentiment? Should ideas or behaviour that hurt a particular intellectual position or group not be banned? Possibly, but a quick resort to bans will chill all debate as everyone will be anguished by ideas they dislike. It is far better to improve the environment for ideas through tolerance and mutual respect.

Let me explain. Actions that physically harm anyone, or show verbal contempt for a particular group so that they damage the group's participation in the marketplace for ideas, should certainly not be allowed. For example, sexual harassment, whether physical or verbal, has no place in society. At the same time, groups should not be looking for slights any and everywhere, so that too much is seen as offensive; the theory of confirmation bias in psychology suggests that once one starts looking for insults, one can find them everywhere, even in the most innocuous statements. Indeed, if what you do offends me but does not harm me otherwise, there should be a very high bar for prohibiting your act. After all, any ban, and certainly any vigilante acts to enforce it, may offend you as much, or more, than the offence to me. Excessive political correctness stifles progress as much as excessive license and disrespect.

Put differently, while you should avoid pressing the buttons that upset me to the extent possible, when you do push them you should explain carefully why that is necessary so as to move the debate forward, and how it should not be interpreted as a personal attack on me. You have to tread respectfully, assuring me that a challenge to the ideas I hold is necessary for progress. At the same time, I should endeavour to hold few ideas so closely intertwined with my personality that any attack on them is deemed an intolerable personal affront. Tolerance means not being so insecure about one's ideas that one cannot subject them to challenge—it implies a degree of detachment that is absolutely necessary for mature debate. Finally, respect requires that in the rare case when an idea is tightly associated with a group's core personality, we are extra careful about challenging it.

Tolerance can take the offence out of debate, and indeed instil respect. If I go berserk every time a particular button is pressed, rebels are tempted to press the button, while mischief-makers indeed do so. But if I do not react predictably, and instead ask button pressers to explain their concerns, rebels are forced to do the hard work of marshalling arguments. So, rebels do not press the button frivolously, while the thuggish mischief makers who abound in every group are left without an easy trigger. Tolerance and respect then lead to a good equilibrium where they reinforce each other.

For example, rebellious youth in the United States used to burn the American flag. It was calculated to upset the older generation that had fought in America's wars, for the flag was a symbol of all they had fought for. And the police, many of whom were veterans, used to react with violence, which was precisely the reaction the rebels sought to further their cause. Over time, though, U.S. society has become more tolerant of flag-burning. Because it no longer triggers a reaction, it is no longer used as an instrument to shock. In sum, if group sentiment becomes more tolerant and less easily hurt, the actions that try to hurt it will diminish. As Mahatma Gandhi said, 'The golden rule of conduct is mutual toleration, seeing that we will never all think alike and we shall always see Truth in fragments and from different points of vision.'

Let me conclude. IITians like you will lead India's race for ideas. The India that you will graduate into is much more capable of using your technological prowess than the India we graduated into. I wish you unlimited ambition, and forecast great success for those of you who continue thinking and challenging. But as you go out in the world, remember our tradition of debate in an environment of respect and tolerance. By upholding it, by fighting for it, you will be repaying your teachers in this great institution, and your parents who worked so hard to send you here. And you will be doing our country a great patriotic service. Thank you and good luck.

## PARO ANAND

### And So We Learn to Hate

*Dhaka, 2017*

*Paro Anand (b. 1957) is a writer for young adults and adults. She has received a number of awards for her writing, including the Bal Sahitya Puraskar. Her books are read in schools and have appeared on many international lists of best books for children and young adults. Paro believes passionately in bringing the voices of the marginalized and neglected into her works. She hopes to create a more inclusive world through her writings. She gave this speech at the Dhaka Literature Festival in 2017.*

Several years ago, in a Delhi school, a voice, bright and confident, wafted up at me, 'I *hate* Muslims,' the child said. The words flew up at me and pierced me like an arrow. I leant out to see what was happening and saw a group of six or so teens. They all nodded in agreement. Yes, they seemed to confirm that they all hated Muslims too. My eyes travelled just beyond the group. One child stood stock still. Rooted to the spot and pale. It was obvious that he was Muslim and that he had heard what his classmates had said. What it must have felt like to him to hear this. Could he even go home and tell his parents or was he going to wrap himself in 'shame'.

Years later, the sentiment remains and grows. The hearts and minds of our young are being corrupted by what I call 'heard prejudice'. They hear adults around them spouting these words and parrot them back without really bothering to ask why. And so they learn Hate.

I knew this was something I had to write. And so was born the story, 'Those Yellow Flowers in August', featured in *Like Smoke* (Penguin), the winner of the Sahitya Akademi, Bal Sahitya Puruskar. The story and indeed the book, starts with the lines, 'I hate Muslims...' People are shocked and mistake these words for mine. But they are not, the character speaks these words after her father is killed by what she is told is a 'Muslim bomb'. The story starts there, but it ends in exactly the opposite place. With her falling in love with a Muslim boy who explains, 'Bombs don't have a religion, violence doesn't have a religion and all Muslims are not terrorists.'

I was telling this story in a school in Rajasthan and after it finished, during Q&A, one young boy said, 'Ma'am, I will agree with you that all Muslims are not terrorists, but you will have to agree with me that almost all terrorists are Muslims. So, what do you have to say about that?' It's a common question that many of us have heard or even asked.

I was lucky that an answer came to me so I countered, 'All right, let's put aside religion for a moment, let's look at another kind of violence, let's take rape as an example.

I think we all agree that all men are not rapists, but you will have to agree with me that almost all rapists are men. So, taking your logic, we should look at all men as potential rapists and treat them with hatred and suspicion. Which means that I should treat you, son, as a potential rapist too, though I know nothing at all about you.'

There was a shocked silence. The boy's fists clenched. He was so upset by my 'accusation'. And then, after a moment or two, I saw the penny drop, a realization. It was a magical collective moment as the auditorium burst into thunderous applause and the students were on their feet. As I was leaving, this same boy came up to me and said that no one had ever explained it to him in a way that he really 'got it'.

Hate had been absorbed by young people. In their homes, in their schools, amongst peers.

Stories, I have seen, are a powerful tool for young people to talk about these issues and see them from perspectives other than their own. Stories can certainly heal wounds and open hearts. It is time to take children's literature very seriously.